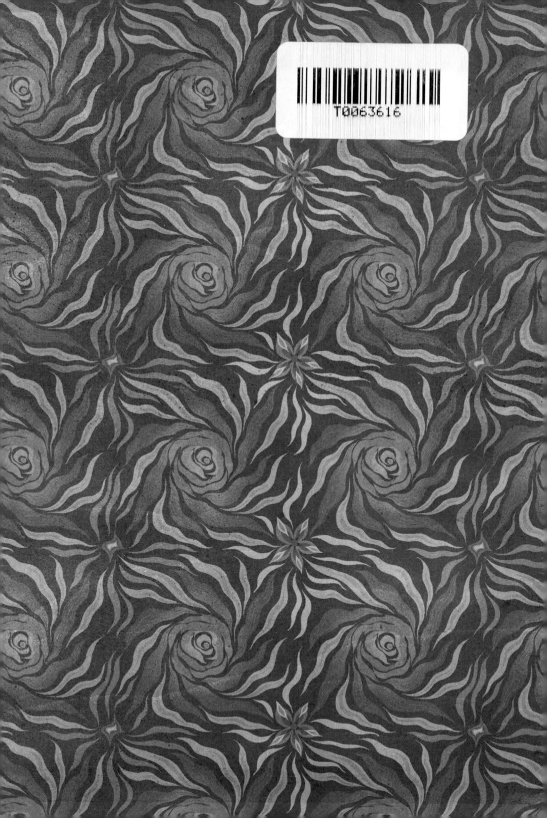

DREAM ON

DREAM ON

A Kid's Guide to
INTERPRETING
DREAMS

CERRIDWEN GREENLEAF
Illustrated by KHOA LE

RP|KIDS
PHILADELPHIA

Running Press Kids
Hachette Book Group
1290 Avenue of the Americas, New York, NY 10104
www.runningpress.com/rpkids
@RP_Kids

Printed in China

First Edition: December 2022

Published by Running Press Kids, an imprint of Perseus Books, LLC,
a subsidiary of Hachette Book Group, Inc. The Running Press Kids name and logo
are trademarks of the Hachette Book Group.

The Hachette Speakers Bureau provides a wide range of authors for speaking events.
To find out more, go to www.hachettespeakersbureau.com or call (866) 376-6591.

The publisher is not responsible for websites (or their content)
that are not owned by the publisher.

Print book cover and interior design by Frances J. Soo Ping Chow.

Library of Congress Cataloging-in-Publication Data
Names: Greenleaf, Cerridwen, author. | Le, Khoa, 1982–illustrator.
Title: Dream on: a kid's guide to interpreting dreams / Cerridwen Greenleaf;
illustrated by Khoa Le. Description: First Edition. | Philadelphia : Running Press, 2022.
| Includes index. Identifiers: LCCN 2021055204 | ISBN 9780762479269 (hardcover)
| ISBN 9780762479276 (ebook) Subjects: LCSH: Dreams—Juvenile literature. |
Subconsciousness—Juvenile literature. | Rapid eye movement sleep—Juvenile literature.
Classification: LCC BF1078 .G754 2022 | DDC 154.6/3—dc23/eng/20220125
LC record available at https://lccn.loc.gov/2021055204

ISBNs: 978-0-7624-7926-9 (hardcover), 978-0-7624-7927-6 (ebook)

1010

10 9 8 7 6 5 4 3 2 1

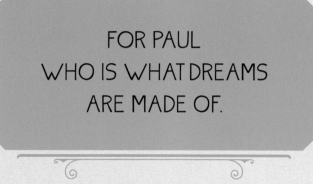

FOR PAUL
WHO IS WHAT DREAMS
ARE MADE OF.

"I HAVE
HAD A VISION.
I HAD
A DREAM. . ."

—WILLIAM SHAKESPEARE

CONTENTS

Introduction
YOUR GUIDE TO DREAMLAND
How to Use This Book

D REAMS ARE AN INVITATION TO GET TO KNOW YOURSELF, understand your mind more fully, and—ultimately—to *be* who you are. Think of this book as an all-access pass to your imagination and the previously unknown realm of the inner workings of your brain. The human brain is a wild and wonderful thing, a rich and vast resource of ideas, memories, meanings, thoughts, and, obviously, dreams. This guide is a toolbox you can open to help you recognize the types of dreams you have, discover patterns of frequent and repeated dreams, and identify messages from your subconscious. Your mind is a treasure chest and one of your greatest gifts. Once you start to unpack what your sleeping mind is processing, you will have a much deeper understanding of yourself and the people in your lives. You'll also learn how to better navigate school, friendships, and activities, as well as recognize helpful signs to stay on course in life.

Starting with the how and why of dreams and the science of sleep, you'll explore this hidden realm of the night. Dreams are no small thing either: they can be a gentle reminder from your brain or a nudge to be more aware of a situation. They can be life-changing and lead to major inventions and breakthrough ideas, as you'll discover in "Dreams That Changed the World." They can be inspiring and offer opportunities for DIY crafts as you'll find in "Dream It (or Do It) Yourself." Whatever dreams you experience, let this book guide you to better understand what's really going on in your mind!

Chapter 1

TO SLEEP, PERCHANCE TO DREAM: DREAM THEORY AND SLEEP SCIENCE

WHY DO WE DREAM?

JUST WHAT EXACTLY IS A DREAM? AS YOU KNOW FROM YOUR own, they consist of seemingly random images, feelings, and fleeting thoughts that come into your mind while you are sleeping. Some we remember, but many we don't. The feelings that dreams create can range from very happy and exciting to sad, stressful, and downright scary. Dreams can be intense! Some dreams are almost like movies with complete story lines. Others—including so many of mine!—seem to make no sense at all and sort of flit from scene to scene, often in a way that has no obvious connection. Or do they?

If, like me, you want to understand it all a bit better, starting with the science behind dreams can help. According to research, every time we sleep for at least ninety minutes, we dream. Even if you wake up not remembering your dreams, it doesn't mean you didn't have any. Our dreaming occurs in phases: waking, light sleep, deep sleep, Rapid Eye Movement (REM) sleep, and repeat. The three phases before REM are referred to as Non-Rapid Eye Movement (NREM) and are more commonly called "quiet sleep." REM is known as "active sleep" and involves faster breathing, eye movement, and your brain being more energetic as well. The dreams we recall happen during this phase of REM sleep, and it seems that this is when we have our most intense dreams. During REM sleep, the brain immobilizes the body; otherwise, we would act out our dreams!

But why do we dream at all? While there are many theories, the most common include:

- To process feelings
- To merge memories
- To manage wants and longings
- To "warn" our waking mind of problems or threats

Why, dear reader, do *you* think we dream?

One of the most famous psychologists of all time, Dr. Sigmund Freud, developed a theory that dreams symbolize our hidden longings, needs, and the fulfillment of our wishes. He believed many of us hide or repress our desires for fear of being judged. Dreams would then serve as a way to process and handle feelings and emotions and also release stress. One long-term impact of Freud's work is that he popularized the interpretation of dreams, which we enjoy and puzzle over even now.

DREAMS PROCESS INFORMATION

After waking up from a dream, our minds take all the images and memories and try to piece them together like a puzzle so that the dream makes sense. The activation-synthesis hypothesis is the formal name of an idea that claims our dreams are really just all sorts of random nonsense—signals and sensory experiences passing through the subconscious as a result of changes in neuron activity. The brain is just trying to create meaning from a bunch of different signals.

DREAMS SUPPORT YOUR MEMORY

Some scientists believe that dreaming is really just taking lots of different information and deciding what is important enough to keep in the memory bank. We take in so much information every day—at school, hanging out with friends, reading books, talking to people, watching movies, shows, or playing video games. Our brains need to sort out all of our life experiences. This particular idea is known as the information processing theory, and many people believe this is the primary reason why humans dream. Some people work with this theory and use dream time to practice complicated tasks or ponder problems and wake up with a solution. Why not try it yourself?

YOUR DREAMS ARE A LAB

Have you ever gone to sleep thinking about a project or problem where the right idea, words, or answer just won't come to you? You wake up in the morning and—bingo!—your mind came up with the exact inspiration you needed. That's because your mind is a mighty problem-solving machine. The creativity theory suggests that once you are asleep, your mind can fly free and be as wildly imaginative as is needed. These "aha" moments in the morning can really help you with schoolwork or dealing with friend or family drama.

YOUR DREAMS ARE A JOURNAL

A relatively new theory of dreams is that they are a reflection of your life, a recording of sorts. This is called the continuity hypothesis, and it is the idea that your dreams bring all your real-life experiences into play. So, in other words, dreaming is something like a pieced-together patchwork of memory fragments. You may awaken and discover that your mind pointed out the importance of something that happened in your life by highlighting the event in your dreams. This may even make sure the happening goes into your long-term memory since it was emphasized in this way.

YOUR DREAMS ARE WARNING YOU

Some psychologists and researchers believe that dreams helped early peoples survive. One of the ways primitive people were able to avoid sabertoothed tigers and mastodons was by dreaming about these dangerous beasts. The unconscious mind was making sure cave dwellers were on high alert to the perils in their environment. Some sleep experts believe that such behaviors actually sharpen our fight-or-flight instincts and can also make you mentally stronger so you can handle what comes your way. Examples of these dreams include:

- Being chased
- Falling from a great height
- Forgetting something of life-and-death importance
- Forgetting to study for a major test
- Forgetting to put on clothes and being caught naked

FURTHER IDEAS
ON WHY WE DREAM

Humans have been dreaming since we came into existence. Therefore, there are many ideas to explain the function of dreams in our lives. Which of these theories do you believe?

The brain is like a computer: it is deleting files that are no longer needed, sort of scrubbing your mind and decluttering so it is fresh and ready for new memories in the morning. Here's to clearing the mental clutter!

A theory called continual-activation is that dreaming keeps our brain sharp so it can function really well and keep recording new memories and new learning so you can be both smart and safe.

A somewhat more direct concept is that dreams are simply our brains processing outer stimuli such as music, a bird's song, a person shouting, or anything that might require you to respond in the best way. A great example is a parent needing to hear a baby's cry to feed or protect the baby. Their brains will wake them up in the middle of the night so they can care for their infant. Sometimes they hear crying in their dreams, which alerts them to wake up.

A very counterintuitive idea called reverse-learning theory is an intriguing one—we dream to forget! Neuroscientists point out that we have zillions of neural connections in what we have stored in our brains—stuff learned at school, from books, our memories—and there is just too much to hold on to, so this concept is that our dreams are sorting out what needs to be kept and what can be forgotten forever.

DREAMS HELP US WITH
ALL THE FEELS

Our dreams are like a lab where our brain tests out emotions and enables us to process them in a healthy way. This is called the emotional regulation theory, and researchers claim that this is the main function of dreams—to support us in coping with our feelings and, most importantly, the really difficult ones such as loss, grief, trauma, sadness, and those *feels* that are an unavoidable part of life. Your dreaming mind is a safe space where you can somehow practice for what you might encounter in real life. I am sure you have had emotionally charged dreams in your REM sleep and woke up thinking it was all real. These vivid dreams are your brain at work.

Do you share your dreams with others and talk about them? I suggest you do, as neuroscientists—those who specialize in how our brains work—have discovered a high degree of empathy in those who discuss their dreams with family and friends. This is yet another way in which dreams are really good for us!

⟫——ε— *fun fact!* —℥——⟪
The world record for the longest a person has ever gone
without sleep is 264 hours.

LUCID DREAMS

Have you ever had a dream where you know you are asleep and can direct your dreams? This kind of dream is known as a lucid dream. They are rare, and scientists are still trying to understand them. It does sound pretty great to be able to control your dream and make it play out as you want. There are even training courses where you can learn to become a lucid dreamer. Some people compare this to experiencing a real-life video game. May all your dreams be happy ones!

ANXIETY DREAMS

When we are under stress, which is all too common nowadays, it can show up when we go to sleep at night. Anxiety or stress dreams are like nightmares and can cause us to wake up upset, sad, or even a little bit scared. Not to worry, Dear Reader: this is yet another way your dreaming mind is protecting you so you can process whatever is bothering you in life and deal with the emotions in the safe space of your dreamscape. Dreams can help you cope with what is going on in your life!

Chapter 2
DREAMS THAT
CHANGED THE WORLD

←─────◦◉◦─────→

THESE FAMOUS PEOPLE FROM HISTORY ALL HAD DREAMS that ended up making an amazing impact! As they slept, their brains continued thinking, imagining, and creating, and the dreams that came from those thoughts led to some amazing creations and discoveries. It just goes to show what a wonderful, mysterious thing the subconscious mind is!

PAUL McCARTNEY

The Beatles' song "Yesterday"—considered by many people to be one of the greatest of all time—started with a dream. Paul McCartney composed the melody of the song in his sleep—can you imagine? He woke up and went straight to the piano to try and replicate it while it was still fresh in his mind. "I just fell out of bed, found out what key I had dreamed it in . . . and I played it," he said. At first, he didn't believe the song he had heard in his dream was actually his own; he thought he had just recalled someone else's song in his dream. For weeks he played the chords for other people in the industry to see if anyone recognized it, but when no one claimed the melody, McCartney began crafting this dream song into what would eventually become "Yesterday." When it was released, it topped the Billboard Hot 100 chart for weeks. It was one of the highest-earning songs of its time and has endured and continued to be covered by big-name artists from around the world to this day.

SRINIVASA RAMANUJAN

Srinivasa Ramanujan was a genius self-taught mathematician, who contributed enormously to his field. He loved math and showed great promise from a very young age. (Side note: he actually flunked out of college because he was so focused on mathematics that he didn't study any other subjects with the same passion.) He even had visions of complicated equations and formulas in his dreams. To this day his findings are being used to solve new challenges in the field of science.

MARY SHELLEY

Mary Shelley was inspired by a vivid nightmare she had one cold winter's night to write the unforgettable novel *Frankenstein*, which cemented her name in history as the mother of science fiction. She had traveled to a villa in Switzerland, just off Lake Geneva, with the famous poets Percy Shelley (her future husband) and Lord Byron. They could hardly go outside because it was so cold, so they amused themselves one dark and chilly evening by reading each other ghost stories! That was when Lord Byron came up with the idea that each of them should write their own horror stories. During that very trip, Mary had a nightmare of a man-made body lying on the floor, stirring and slowly taking on a life of its own as its creator kneeled over it. It was such a frightening dream that she lay awake the rest of the night, haunted by the images. She was unable to shake the memory the next day, so, naturally, she decided to write about it!

ALBERT EINSTEIN

We all know about Albert Einstein, the German-born scientist who is acknowledged as one of the greatest physicists of all time. But did you know that the bud of his famous theory of relativity may have grown from a dream? One night, he had a dream that he was sledding at night with some friends. In the dream, he slid down a steep hill, and his sled kept going faster and faster until he started to reach light speed! In fact, he was moving so fast that the stars started to look different—from his perspective, they had altered into unfamiliar colors that amazed him. He remained thoughtful about the dream after he woke up, and many believe that this dream was what planted the seed of inspiration that speed affects matter, time, and space.

HARRIET TUBMAN

Harriet Tubman was a hero. During the Civil War she led over seventy enslaved people to freedom as part of the Underground Railroad; worked for the Union army as a cook, nurse, and then spy; and was the very first woman to lead a military operation during the Civil War—one that rescued hundreds more people. But what you might not know about Tubman is that she credited her successful rescue missions to vivid dreams—or visions—she had, which she believed came from God. These dreams, she said, gave her direction and kept her and those she was leading to freedom safe on their journey, guiding them through unfamiliar terrain. She started having visions when she was an adolescent, after being hit in the head while trying to protect a person escaping slavery. It's clear that her powerful intuition was at work even in her sleep.

NIELS BOHR

Niels Bohr was a physicist who is known today as the father of quantum mechanics. He won the Nobel Prize for Physics for discovering the structure of an atom in the year 1922. Bohr said the discovery was the result of a dream he had. One night, during his dream, he saw electrons spinning around the nucleus of an atom, in specific orbits—like the planets in our solar system travel around the sun. The dream inspired him to go to his lab and begin the necessary experiments to confirm his theory. Turns out, all the evidence he gathered supported this structure, and it was all thanks to one inspiring dream!

ROBERT LOUIS STEVENSON

Robert Louis Stevenson conceived the famous novel *Strange Case of Dr. Jekyll and Mr. Hyde* in a dream while he was terribly ill with tuberculosis. After waking up from a nightmare, he was able to remember a few key scenes from the dream and began writing his book about the headstrong scientist and his impulsive alter ego the next day. He finished writing it in about three days, much to the amazement of his family, and the unforgettable work of fiction is all thanks to Stevenson's scary dream.

SALVADOR DALÍ

The famous surrealist painter Salvador Dalí got the inspiration for many of his paintings from dreams! His most iconic work, *The Persistence of Memory*—with its bizarre but mesmerizing melting clocks dripping under the desert sun—was one of these dream paintings. Dalí was able to have lucid dreams, and it was in them that he found a muse for his art. He even described his paintings as "hand-painted dream photographs," which feels like a perfect summary of his work—he painted images that accurately characterize the strangeness our dreamscapes so often have. Dalí once said this about dreaming: "One day it will have to be officially admitted that what we have christened reality is an even greater illusion than the world of dreams."

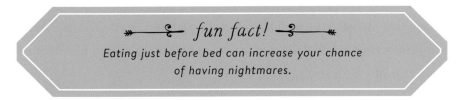

fun fact!
Eating just before bed can increase your chance
of having nightmares.

FREDERICK BANTING

Frederick Banting revolutionized medicine by discovering a treatment for diabetes, and it was all thanks to a dream. Diabetes was a death sentence at the time, and Banting—driven by his mother's death from that same disease—wanted to find a way to cure people suffering with it. He didn't find an end-all cure, but he *did* discover a way to treat diabetes patients that would save their lives—and that continues to do so today. Banting knew the pancreas was involved somehow, and after reading himself to sleep with articles about the organ one night, he had a dream about an experiment. He described a research proposal based on it to his colleagues, and he and his research team set to work. As a result of their experiments, they were able to discover an imbalance between sugar and insulin in diabetic patients. They eventually created an insulin injection that could be given to people with diabetes!

MADAM C. J. WALKER

Madam C. J. Walker was the first American woman to become a self-made millionaire. She was an African American businesswoman, philanthropist, and activist who created her own company selling hair products. She went from laundress to saleswoman, working for another hair-care company until she developed a product of her very own that would rocket her to fame. All her life she had struggled with scalp infections, dandruff, and hair loss, and so she experimented with a variety of different hair-care products that didn't help—until one day she had a dream that changed the game. Walker claimed the formula for her product came to her in her sleep. Some of the ingredients had to be imported from Africa, which required time and money, but it was worth it. After perfecting the formula, Walker went door to door selling the mixture and teaching other Black women how to style and care for their hair. Her business grew from there!

ELIAS HOWE

Elias Howe grew up in Massachusetts during a textile boom, and living near the state's textile mills himself, he ended up becoming a very important person in the industry. He is credited with inventing the sewing machine, and although he wasn't actually the first person to come up with the idea, he did create and patent the lockstitch design that played a key role in improving the automated sewing process. And it was all because of a dream! There are a few different versions of the story, but one is that he dreamed he had to build a sewing machine for a wicked king but couldn't come up with the right design for the needle—just like in his waking life. The king gave him a short amount of time to find a solution, or be executed. When Howe couldn't think of anything, the king's warriors came for him with their spears. As he looked at the shining spears, he suddenly had an idea. The spears had a hole at the tip. All Howe needed to do was recreate that with a needle. He woke up from his dream and rushed to try out his new idea, and from there he was finally able to complete the design that would revolutionize sewing.

Chapter 3
DREAM IT
(OR DO IT) YOURSELF

GOING TO SLEEP AT NIGHT CAN BE LIKE ENTERING AN
enchanted realm. Here are a few tried-and-true crafts you can
try to better connect with your dreams so that you wake up happier and have more of whatever you want in your life—success at school,
a peaceful and joyful home, and even more love in your life.

MAKE YOUR OWN DREAM JOURNAL

Pick out a really cool notebook or blank journal and grab some glitter,
colorful pens, ribbons, and stickers galore so you can customize your very
own dream journal.

Keep it by your bed with a pen or pencil and write down your dreams
when you wake up. Even the very ordinary dreams that seem a bit boring
should go in there. Pay attention to any patterns or imagery that keeps
appearing in your dreams. How did each dream make you feel? Note
that, too. What will you discover about yourself from this new activity of
dream journaling?

SWEET DREAMS BATH SOAK

If you've been having trouble sleeping lately, this bath bomb will have you in a deep slumber.

Gather together:

1 cup Epsom salts

1 cup baking soda

12 drops clary sage essential oil

12 drops lavender essential oil

8 drops jasmine oil

Mixing bowl and wooden spoon

Sealable jar or canister

Combine Epsom salts and baking soda in the bowl with the wooden spoon and then add in the essential oils and blend well. Take a handful of mixture and roll it in your palms to create a ball. Repeat until all the mixture has been used. Store the bath bombs in a resealable jar. This is enough for about four baths for whenever you need a respite from the worries of the world.

A GOOD NIGHT'S SLEEP SACHET

The sweet scent of flower petals and herbs can bring deep rest,
making you feel more energized every morning.

Gather together:

A small cloth bag with string to tie it
Fresh white and pink rose petals, ½ cup
Dried woolly thyme, ⅓ cup
A pinch of ground cinnamon
A vanilla bean
A piece of white paper and a pen
A white quartz crystal

Mix the flowers and herbs together, and fill the bottom half of the bag. Chop the vanilla bean with a table knife and add that in. Now write down two to three things you want to feel after sleep. For example, maybe you want to feel relaxed or you want to have more energy. Fold the paper at least once to fit it into the bag. Fill the rest of the bag with more of the flower and herb mix. Nestle the crystal in the herbs right at the top and tie the bag. Each night, take a sniff of the bag before you place it under your pillow to remind you of your search for true restoration.

QUIET MIND MEDITATION

Try this before you go to bed when you are stressed or have a big day planned so you are calm and ready for anything the next morning! All you need is a clear quartz crystal or a pretty white stone you find in your path.

Meditation is surprisingly easy. First, get comfortable and sit down on the floor or in a chair with both feet flat on the floor. I suggest taking a deep breath and exhaling slowly. I do it five times in five deep breaths. After that, empty your mind. All the worries about homework, band practice, mom's birthday gifts, and *everything* else, just put it aside and clear your mind. At first, your mind may wander a bit—it happens to all of us—but just keep focusing on your breathing and nothing else. Short intervals of eleven minutes are a good way to start. Like anything else in life, practice makes perfect!

Sit up and listen for the first thing that comes into your mind—it should be the answer or a message regarding any issue or problem that is causing you stress. The next morning, you will feel more rested and prepared to face the day ahead.

>> —&— *fun fact!* —&— «

Most people can only dream about faces they've seen before, so even if you don't recognize a person in your dream, it's probably still someone you know!

DIY DREAM CATCHER

You can create a simple dream catcher or wind chime
from your own collection of rocks, old keys, crystals, and shiny
objects anytime you want to gather up good dreams.

Supplies:

String

Chunks of crystals, old keys, etc.

A small stick

Tie string around the pieces of crystal, keys, or other objects you've gathered.

Attach each string to your stick of wood.

Hang your dream catcher/wind chime in your home or your bedroom window.

MELLOW OUT MIST

Make your own sleep mist that you can spray
on your pillow as part of your bedtime routine!

Gather together:

3 drops rose oil

3 drops lavender oil

3 drops neroli, orange blossom essence

4 ounces pure distilled water

Pour all these into a colored glass spray bottle and shake well three times. Fifteen minutes before you get in bed, spray lightly on your sheets and pillowcase.

QUIZ

WHAT DO YOUR DREAMS SAY ABOUT YOU?

Which of these things or events appear
in your dreams most often?

ROUND 1

A. Getting caught in a huge wave

B. Going on a date

C. Jumping really high

D. Riding in an airplane

ROUND 2

A. Swimming in the ocean

B. Traveling

C. Being able to fly

D. Climbing uphill

ROUND 3

A. Boats

B. Motorcycles

C. Feet

D. Cars

ROUND 4

A. Fish

B. Horses

C. Cats

D. Birds

ROUND 5

A. Drowning

B. Dancing

C. Running in a race

D. Visiting the mountains

IF YOU ANSWERED MOSTLY A'S . . . YOU'RE AN EMOTIONAL PERSON. You feel very deeply and care a lot about others. You probably tend to notice and absorb the emotions of the people around you. You are all about being present and experiencing everything that comes your way, and you are very in tune with your emotions. However, because you feel so strongly, sometimes you can get overwhelmed by your own feelings.

IF YOU ANSWERED MOSTLY B'S . . . YOU'RE AN ADVENTUROUS PERSON. You are excited to try new things and are always looking for a good adventure. You take everything in stride and aren't afraid when life throws a new curveball your way. You follow your passions and crave new experiences, whether that's taking up hobbies, traveling to places you've never been, or following your curiosity wherever it takes you. You might even be a bit of a daredevil! This means you can also be a bit too reckless at times.

IF YOU ANSWERED MOSTLY C'S . . . YOU'RE A CAREFREE PERSON. You value freedom and don't care too much about what others think of you. You take life each day at a time, without worrying too much about what tomorrow will bring, and you express yourself freely. You are almost always true to yourself and rarely feel like you have to pretend to be someone you're not. You are independent, and don't need to rely on anyone else to make you feel valued and important. Your carefree attitude can also mean that you sometimes avoid letting yourself be tied down by duty or that you neglect your responsibilities.

IF YOU ANSWERED MOSTLY D'S . . . YOU'RE AN AMBITIOUS PERSON. You are very driven and know exactly what you want, and you'll do whatever it takes to reach your goals. You never back down from a challenge, especially when you know that there's a big reward on the other side. You feel confident in your ability to succeed and will probably go on to do big things and make an impact on the world. Sometimes you push yourself too hard, however, so make sure you are taking time for yourself to rest and recharge.

Chapter 4
EMBARRASSING DREAMS

YOU KNOW EXACTLY WHAT WE'RE TALKING ABOUT HERE. You are fast asleep having one of the worst moments of your life, but it feels so real! Who knows why our dreaming minds produce such humiliation, but it might be related to the same theory that says primitive peoples dreamed about the sorts of wild animals that might attack them when they emerged from their caves. These nightmarish scenarios we experience in our sleep help make sure we don't forget important things when awake—like wearing pants! I suggest you take these with a big grain of salt, keep your sense of humor about things, and try to glean how this forewarning applies to your life. Just remember that your brain is your friend, and you'll be fine!

BEING NAKED IN PUBLIC

You're going about your day—walking to school, shopping at the mall, riding the bus, or what have you—when suddenly you look down to see that you are completely *naked*. Maybe you duck behind a tree or desperately search your backpack for something to cover up with. This is a particularly common dream, and it can have a variety of meanings depending on the context. It is important to recognize the feelings you associate with your dream, as this will help you uncover its meaning.

Most often, naked dreams are associated with feelings of insecurity. Nudity represents vulnerability—your clothes act as a shield to protect you, and once that shield is gone, you may feel exposed and defenseless. In your waking life you may be too concerned about how others perceive you, or perhaps you are in a situation that is making you feel helpless. Nudity might also indicate there is something in your life you are trying to hide from the people around you. If you are in a situation where you are hoping to impress others, your dream might be telling you that you are trying to be someone you're not. You aren't being true to yourself, and you fear that if the people around you find out who you really are, they might judge you.

Being naked in your dream can be a hint that you are unprepared for something as well. Do you feel unprepared for a school project? A test? There may be something in your waking life that has caught you off guard and is causing you anxiety. Your subconscious might even be trying to tell you that you're holding yourself to a standard that is too high to meet.

Usually, in these dreams, you will rarely find anyone noticing you are undressed. They are all going about their usual business without giving you a second thought—which implies that your fears are likely unfounded. You don't need to be afraid of what others think of you; trust in yourself and your abilities and have confidence in who you are.

WEARING THE WRONG CLOTHES

Clothes symbolize the version of yourself that you show to other people or how others perceive you. If you have a dream where you are dressed inappropriately—whether that's wearing a wedding dress to a baseball game or gym clothes to the school dance—your subconscious might be trying to tell you that it's time to stop worrying about how others see you and start expressing yourself more freely. We tend to dress up based on what sort of image we want to show to other people, but in putting up this sort of front, you might be stifling your own individuality—trading who you really are for who you think everyone else wants you to be.

What your clothes feel like in your dreams can tell you something about yourself as well: too-tight clothes are a sign there is something in your waking life that is holding you back, while clothes that are too loose can indicate you are feeling inadequate. It is possible that you are also in a situation you feel unprepared for.

SHOWING UP LATE TO SOMETHING

Dreaming about being late often means that you are unconsciously experiencing fear of missing out (FOMO). If you lost out on an important opportunity in your real life, your dream might be a reflection of that frustration. It's also possible that part of you is feeling left behind: maybe there are milestones in your life you haven't experienced yet or

expectations you had for things that haven't played out the way you'd hoped. Maybe you worry you've fallen behind your friends. These days we can experience a lot of pressure from friends, family, and society, and when we see others achieving wonderful things, we can start to feel inadequate. Your dream may be trying to tell you to slow down and focus on where you are in your life right now instead of worrying about what lies ahead.

A dream about being late could also be a wake-up call for you. Have you been letting opportunities slip away because you feel like you aren't good enough? Is there a relationship in your life that needs developing? This dream might be a sign that it's time to pull yourself together and step out of your comfort zone before you let something good pass you by. Perhaps it's time to reevaluate your priorities.

NOT BEING ABLE TO FIND A BATHROOM

This dream is one that is often associated with worry or anxiety. Quite often, having a dream about not being able to find a bathroom means there is something in your life that it's time to let go of, something you may be struggling to release. There may be a situation that is bringing negativity into your life, something that is weighing on you, or simply an overwhelming number of responsibilities to tend to. The toilet represents a very basic need in the human life and can indicate that you are not caring for your own emotional or physical needs. Consider the things that may be causing fear in your waking life. Is there something you are holding on to that is only hurting you in the long run?

Loosen your grip on the things that disrupt your peace of mind and prepare to walk away from old lifestyle patterns that are leading you away from growth.

FAILING A TEST

Taking a test in a dream is often a sign of a challenge in your waking life, something that has put you under pressure or is causing the people in your life to analyze you. Perhaps you actually have an upcoming exam in real life that is causing you anxiety, or maybe the "test" in your dream is a representation of some other trial you have had to face. Tests often symbolize being unprepared and can reflect anxiety for the future as well as guilt about the past. Did you back down from a challenge? There may be another lying in wait for you. In these dreams, people often feel like they are running out of time, or they can't understand the questions, or their pencil keeps breaking and preventing them from finishing.

The feelings you experience while taking the test in your dream can reflect your confidence in your waking life. If you are failing a test or wallowing in the fear of failing, you may be struggling with self-esteem. You likely have all the tools you need to succeed, but are selling yourself short, or you are setting goals that are too high, and as a result, you fear not being able to meet your own standards.

Consider your attitude toward things that are giving you difficulties in life. Do you find yourself always considering the worst possible scenario? Are you constantly trying to prove yourself to the people in your life? Evaluating these thoughts and feelings in your waking life will help you better understand what your dream is pointing to.

»—— ——ᷤ— *fun fact!* —ᶾ —— «

You can learn while you sleep! Our brains continue to learn and reorganize memories even while we are unconscious. We can practice problem-solving even in our dreams, and if we are learning something new when we are awake, getting a good night's sleep can help those skills and information sink in.

BACK TO SCHOOL WOES

When we have dreams about going back to school, it may be a sign that there are some life lessons still to be learned. It is time to think about what our experiences have taught us and what we may have missed along the way. These dreams can often be very tense, involving negative events like getting lost in school, not being able to find your locker, or missing a class. This might be your unconscious showing you that you've lost your way in your waking life.

Try to think of areas in your life where you feel you aren't progressing. It could be a situation where you responded immaturely or unhealthy habits that you need to unlearn. Your dream could also be encouraging you to pursue new knowledge. After all, learning is something that should happen throughout your life, not just during the school day.

PERFORMING IN PUBLIC

Dreams about performing onstage or in a public place can have slightly different interpretations depending on how comfortable you are both in your dream and in your waking life with that sort of thing. Often the audience can represent your social circles: peers that could include friends, family, or classmates. A happy audience that is cheering for you may show that you feel your efforts are always well received and you are liked and appreciated in your circles, while a negative reaction might mean you are uncomfortable with these people and feel overly judged.

Performing onstage can also be a sign that you are trying to win over your peers by showing them only the best sides of yourself—and while this might get you praise and recognition, you might only be letting people get to know you on a very superficial level. Think about your waking life. Are you afraid that if you show others your genuine self you might face rejection? If you want to get closer to the people in your life, it may be time to stop trying so hard to impress them and instead show them a more authentic version of yourself.

Chapter 5
HAPPY DREAMS

Have you ever woken up from a dream and wished you could just fall back asleep and pick up right where you left off? Those are exactly the kind of dreams we're talking about in this chapter. Positive dreams are usually a great sign about your self-esteem and mental health, so go you! Keep taking good care of yourself and share some of that joyful energy from your dream life with those around you.

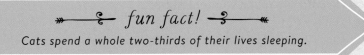

fun fact!
Cats spend a whole two-thirds of their lives sleeping.

GOING ON VACATION

Picture the wind blowing through your hair, sand under your toes, waves crashing in the distance . . . now *that's* the kind of dream you'd like to never wake up from. If you're having dreams about going on a nice vacation, whether to a foreign country, the beach, or a mountain retreat, your subconscious mind might be expressing a craving for a *real* vacation. If you've been bogged down with school, chores, or other commitments recently, it may be wise to take a break. Give yourself some time to do something that revitalizes your spirit. Focus on slowing down—you've done enough and it's time to recharge.

FINDING MONEY

Money is a symbol of prosperity, nourishment, satisfaction, and confidence. Coming upon money in your dreams is usually a good sign—some might even consider it to be an omen that good things are about to come your way! Usually, however, riches in dreams are rarely connected to real-world money. Instead, they indicate a wealth of positivity in your life: an abundance of kindness, friendships, wisdom, and love. Anything that is particularly valuable to you, anything you treasure, might be represented in your dream in the form of money. Are things in your life going well for you? Are you surrounded by people who care about you? Perhaps you received high marks on your last test or scored the winning goal for your team. Any of these things can prompt such a dream. If, however, you haven't been feeling quite so lucky, this dream might be a sign for you to remember all of the good things that you *do* have. What things in your life make you feel rich?

HAVING SUPERPOWERS

If you're having dreams about gaining superpowers, it's often a sign that you are feeling empowered—you know exactly what you are capable of and you have the drive and the confidence to put yourself out there and get things done. This dream can be interpreted as a sign that things are going well for you and you have a positive self-image, in which case, keep it up! It is important that we learn to trust ourselves and be confident in our ability to succeed. Additionally, if you've become a superhero in your dream, that can indicate you have a strong sense of justice and are doing your part to make the world a better place. Your boldness and concern for others will make you a great advocate for those whose voices are not being heard.

TRAVELING BACK IN TIME

Whether there are time machines involved or you simply find yourself revisiting a certain moment of your life, traveling back in time symbolizes fondness for the past and even a desire to recreate some of the feelings you experienced back then. This dream is usually a positive one and gives you the chance to reflect on how far you have come in life and on all the good things that have brought you to where you are today. As wonderful as the past may be, it's important not to get stuck in it, though. If you are experiencing frustration with your current life, try taking steps to create more positive experiences now and lean into the new: new relationships, new activities, etc. The past is in the past, and the present is here for you to enjoy. Things will never be the same as they were, and if you are cling-ing to that idea, you will struggle to be present for all the great things happening in your life today.

RECEIVING A GIFT

Bows and ribbons and wrapping paper, woo-hoo! Dreaming about receiv-ing and opening presents is usually a sign that you're open-minded and accepting of the people in your life. It can be associated with feelings of gratitude and a sign of your appreciation for someone, or it can indi-cate that you are feeling appreciated in your waking life. Another way of interpreting getting gifts in your dream is that you are getting what you deserve for the kindness and generosity that you've shown to others. Opening gifts can be a symbol of your own self-exploration, too, as you discover new things about yourself or uncover new talents and interests. This dream is definitely a happy one—some would even say that dreams about receiving gifts are a sign that good things are coming your way!

Chapter 6
COMMON NIGHTMARES

＋◦—◦○◦—◦＋

YOU CAN HAVE A TOTALLY PEACEFUL AND AWESOME LIFE, and that still won't keep you from having bad dreams. It is just one of those things that happens to us humans. As we know from the theories covered earlier, it can be your brain's way of warning you or of organizing information. Other researchers think it is a kind of "brain dump," and still others believe it can be your intuition at work or psychic dreams. Any way you slice it, nightmares can be scary, so remember, if one enters your dream space, take Taylor Swift's advice when you wake up and just shake it off!

BEING ABANDONED

The most literal way to interpret this dream is that it could be related to an event from your past or present waking life at a time when you were or just felt abandoned. This dream can also be a sign that you are afraid of being rejected or that you have lost something that meant a lot to you. Maybe a friend has been hanging out with a new group and you're worried about getting left behind. Think about anything that might have happened to make you feel neglected. Take this dream as a sign to focus on healing and moving forward.

SOMEBODY (OR SOMETHING) IS CHASING YOU

This is one of the most common—and most frightening—dreams you can have. It's the sort of chest-pounding, heart-stopping dream that makes you shoot up out of bed, right before the chaser lays their hands (or claws) on you. This dream has to do with feelings of stress and anxiety in your waking life. It can be the result of your brain's fight-or-flight reflex in response to something that is threatening your well-being. Some things you will want to notice in your dream are who or what is chasing you, how you are feeling in the dream, and whether you escape whatever is chasing you.

Chase dreams are also associated with avoidance. A chase dream can mean that you are running from something in your waking life. It could be a situation you don't want to deal with, a friend you need to hold accountable, or a fear that needs to be confronted. Probably, the things that happen in this dream show how you cope when problems and pressures come your way. If you know the person chasing you in your dream, it's possible that you have an ongoing issue with that person in reality. The chaser can also represent some part of yourself or some feelings that you have been keeping down. Let your intuition guide you—chances are you already know what this dream is trying to tell you, you just need to confront the truth. It's time to stop hiding. Once you face the thing(s) you've been avoiding, you will have much more peace of mind.

BEING WATCHED

If you're having dreams about being watched, this can be a sign that you feel like you can't relax because of all the expectations being placed on you. It might be time to set some boundaries. You deserve your privacy and shouldn't have to feel like every little thing you are doing is being judged. It is also possible that something is bothering you that you can't seem to get out of your head—maybe a comment someone made about you or an awkward moment you wish you could do over. Protect yourself and pay attention to the energies that are clinging to you.

DROWNING

Dreams about drowning can be interpreted a few different ways. The most common interpretation is that you are feeling overwhelmed. If there are too many things happening in your life, you may feel like you can hardly take a breath. You might be afraid of losing control—anything from deadlines or a heavy homework load to friend or family drama or responsibilities at home can make you feel trapped. If things in your waking life feel hopeless, this dream can be a sign that you have hit a dead end. Water as a dream symbol is associated with emotion, so think about the feelings that are bogging you down in life and what steps you can take to let go of some of the pressure you're feeling.

On a more positive note, this dream can also symbolize rebirth, which means some exciting changes are ahead. Perhaps you want to take up a new hobby or learn a new language. A new friend in your life is also a positive change. Or you might want to sign up for a fun extracurricular activity at school. This will help you get there!

FALLING

This super common dream usually symbolizes losing control. The terror you might feel in your dream as you fall from a skyscraper, airplane, or mountain path represents the fear you have about managing all the responsibilities in your life. Perhaps you're trying to juggle homework, extracurricular activities, chores, and hanging out with friends. It's a lot. And it's OK if you can't manage it all anymore. Let go of your desire to be in control of every little thing.

Dreams about falling can also be a sign that you are dealing with some insecurity. Is there anything happening in your life that has you questioning your self-worth? If so, remind yourself that you are doing the best you can and that you are worthy of happiness and light.

GETTING TRAPPED OR CRUSHED

If you are having dreams about being crushed under something, trapped in an elevator, or confined in any way, it's probably a sign from your subconscious that there is something in your waking life holding you back. If you're struggling with school, have hit a rough patch in a friendship or relationship, or just feel stuck in a rut, these feelings of frustration can translate into dreams of being literally trapped. Try to identify anything in your waking life that is holding you up. Is it something you have always believed in but now doesn't seem to fit? Relationships you've grown out of but are afraid to let go of? Recognizing whatever it may be is the first step to moving on and creating space for yourself to grow.

COMMITTING A CRIME

Dreaming that you've committed or been found guilty of a crime can be a sign that you are feeling bad about a mistake you made when you were awake. Think about your actions and interactions in the real world. Have you done anything recently that could have hurt one of your friends in some way? Perhaps you said something that offended a family member? If you know you have done something wrong, this dream could also be a sign that you are afraid of the consequences of your actions. Those repercussions will catch up to you sooner or later, so it's time for you to own up to them and make things right.

HAVING SURGERY

Dreams about surgery can be scary, but often, they're related to personal healing. If the dream doesn't have to do with some outside factors—like you or a friend undergoing surgery in real life—then it is probably a teaching moment. Think about what sort of surgery you are having in your dream and what things might be bothering you in your waking life that need to be cut out. Surgeries are meant to help, not hurt you, and in the same way, this dream may be encouraging you to get rid of something unhealthy from your life. Even if the separation is uncomfortable, scary, or painful, it will be better for your physical and emotional well-being in the long run. If you have been struggling with feelings of anxiety in your life, or just general distress, consider what the source might be and what parts of that you can change or carve out of your life. Trust me—it will be a wonderful, cleansing process!

GETTING LOST

Dreaming about getting lost somewhere might be a sign from your subconscious that you have lost direction in your waking life. Perhaps you feel like you don't quite fit in at school, or maybe you just think you are somewhere you don't really belong. Maybe you've surrounded yourself with people that don't suit you, or you're trying to adjust to new surroundings. Because your body and mind are taking time to adapt to these changes, those feelings of being off-balance find their way into your dreams.

It's also possible you have realized that the path you are on is leading you somewhere you don't want to go. Maybe you are being pressured by friends or family to do something that isn't right for you. Maybe you joined a new after-school club that's not really your thing. You could be pushing yourself to be someone you're not so that you can please the authority figures in your life or fit in better at school, and because of this, you've started to lose some of your sense of self.

>>———— *fun fact!* ————<<
Bad dreams are much more common than good ones.
Studies show that we are much more likely to have dreams about
upsetting, dangerous situations than realistic ones.

LOSING SOMETHING

Having dreams about losing something is similar to having dreams about being lost. There is probably something missing from your waking life or something that you are feeling insecure about. Usually the thing you have lost is important, so when trying to interpret the dream, it is the key to figuring out what you're missing. The lost object can be a symbol for a lot of different things. For example, dreaming about losing your locker combination could be a sign that you're feeling insecure about something related to school—one of your classes, perhaps. Dreaming about losing your wallet could be a sign that you aren't being careful with your money. You might be spending your money too recklessly and not saving any for the future. Pay attention to the object that you lost in your dream and think about what kinds of things you associate with that object. If it's a pencil, that could be related to study, intelligence, or creativity. Keys could symbolize a feeling of security or privacy. Shoes can relate to travel, motivation, and a sense of purpose. This dream will mean something different depending on your lost item, how you feel about that item, and how you think the item can connect to events in your waking life.

Chapter 7
CREATURES AND MONSTERS

Y OU CAN'T GET MUCH CREEPIER THAN THIS. DREAMING
about monsters can often feel like a horror movie is playing in
your own mind. But don't worry about bad omens and try not
to take these dreams too seriously. Monsters are fantastical beings, and
here in your dreams they have no power over you unless *you* breathe life
into them. When trying to understand why you're having nightmares, it's
important to consider some of the symbolic implications these beings
might have.

ZOMBIES

If you've been watching or reading lots of zombie stories, they could start
following you into your dreams—but if they start showing up without any
direct connection to something you've seen or heard in your waking life,
this is probably a sign that you're in a place in life where you're feeling
detached from reality and your emotions. Zombies as a dream symbol are
connected to aloofness, repetition, laziness, and mindlessness. If you've
seen a zombie—or multiple ones—in your dream, it might mean that
you are just going through the motions in life. Zombies are half alive,
half dead. They move without direction or motivation, which might par-
allel some of your own feelings. You might be going through life without

really living, letting great chances pass you by because you don't have the motivation to pursue them. It's possible that you are having trouble connecting with the people in your life and have lost your sense of passion. Recognizing the zombie in you is the first step toward rediscovering your enthusiasm for life.

Zombies can also be a sign that you are blindly following others and taking everything you hear as fact without thinking for yourself. If you've been letting other people influence all of your opinions and decisions instead of fighting for the things you believe in, you might feel like you don't have any control over your own life. It's time to ask yourself what you really believe in. What is it that *you* want to do? What kind of person do *you* want to be? If you are fighting or running from zombies in your dream, this can be a sign that you are attempting to run from people trying to control you or that you need to stay strong in the face of peer pressure.

»——❦ *fun fact!* ❧——«

We forget most of our dreams within just a few minutes of waking up! Usually, what we remember is only about 10–50 percent of the dreams we had that night, and even then, most of the details of those dreams are lost after ten minutes of being awake.

VAMPIRES

Vampires are mysterious, alluring, and frightening creatures. Those lurking in our dreams can carry a few different meanings. Your vampire dream should be interpreted mostly on the basis of how you see the vampire and the circumstances of the dream. Are you running from the vampire? Have you become a vampire? Dreams about vampires are often interpreted as a sign there is something in your life that is draining you. Perhaps there is a person or influence in your life that is using you to further their own selfish interests. You might be having a hard time cutting them off, but deep down, part of you knows this person is not good for you and that a continued relationship will only harm you. Be careful that you yourself are not being such an influence on someone else—draining the emotional energy of the people around you to feed yourself.

GHOSTS

Ghosts tend to symbolize something in your life that has been left unresolved. You may have some unfinished business in your waking life or some issues from your past that need to be confronted in order for you to move on. This dream may be a sign for you to seek closure for a past relationship, a friendship that ended, or someone you cared about that you lost. It is possible you have been trying to avoid addressing whatever loose ends you have in waking life, but as much as you work at it, they keep coming back to haunt you. It's time for you to move forward and leave the past in the past, so let this dream be the thing that starts that journey of healing and seek out the resolution you need.

MONSTERS AND DEMONS

Creatures like monsters and demons are usually manifestations of fears that we have in our waking lives. They often appear in our dreams during times of serious stress or anxiety. Maybe there is a deadline looming over you—a project you put off starting or a test you haven't studied for. Is there a specific situation you're dreading? Another possibility is you might be letting negative influences in your life get to you, and the evil beings represent negative thoughts and feelings or insecurities running through your head. You might also be consumed with irrational fears that are taking over your subconscious. It can sometimes help to talk to a friend or teacher or family member who can help you deal with whatever is on your mind.

ALIENS

Aliens symbolize things that are foreign or strange to you, so having a dream about aliens may mean that you are experiencing something new and strange in your waking life. It's possible that you are in a situation that is making you feel alienated, like being the outsider in a new school or friend group, moving to a new town, starting a new school year, or joining a new team in your extracurricular time. Alien dreams can be a sign you're trying to adjust and adapt to a new environment or that you're trying to understand some unfamiliar parts of yourself. You might take this dream as a sign to explore the things that feel unfamiliar to you or to try learning new things, like a foreign language or a hobby.

Think about the feelings you had during this alien encounter in your dream. A scary dream can be a sign of fear about the changing circumstances in your life, while a dream full of wonder and curiosity, such as befriending or communicating with an alien, can be a sign that you are approaching these new circumstances in a healthy manner and that you are taking the time to get used to whatever this unusual part of your waking life is.

THE BEST HEALING STONES FOR YOU BASED ON YOUR MOST COMMON DREAMS

Some people believe there are crystals and stones that lend power to help deal with problems and overcome challenges. This quiz can help you identify which might be your power stones!

Circle the dreams you have most often or think you are most likely to have:

SET 1

A. You are naked in public.

B. You start losing your teeth.

C. You can't find the bathroom.

D. You're driving an out-of-control vehicle.

SET 2

A. Your hair is falling out.

B. You've got glass in your mouth.

C. You're being chased.

D. You're falling.

SET 3

A. The person you're going out with is cheating on you.

B. Your phone is broken.

C. You failed a test.

D. You're drowning.

IF YOU ANSWERED MOSTLY A'S . . . CARNELIAN. These dreams are often a sign that you are struggling with self-esteem and need a little bit of a confidence boost. Carnelian, a stone that is believed to help with courage and confidence, is the perfect one for you. This glittering, translucent red quartz suggests warmth and vitality. Its bold, invigorating energy can help you to overcome your fears and regain your power. Carry it in your pocket for strength.

IF YOU ANSWERED MOSTLY B'S . . . AQUAMARINE. If any of these dreams have been bothering you recently, try keeping an aquamarine on you. Dreams like these are usually a sign that you are having some difficulties with communication, so this gem with its crystal blue sheen is the one for you! Aquamarine is associated with the throat and often used as an aid for communication, so it may help you to express yourself better and communicate more clearly with your family and friends. Keep it near your computer, phone, or other devices you use to communicate; it will help you be a better communicator!

IF YOU ANSWERED MOSTLY C'S . . . AMETHYST. You may be struggling with a lot of anxiety in your waking life. Amethyst is thought to be one of the best stones for stress and anxiety, so if you relate to these dreams, this is the crystal for you. It's calming, just like the various shades of purple it can be found in, and makes for a great healer. Many people even put amethysts under their pillows to help with better sleep!

IF YOU ANSWERED MOSTLY D'S . . . SMOKY QUARTZ. These three dreams usually happen when you feel like you're slightly out of control. You might be feeling lost and helpless or out of touch with reality. If this sounds like you, smoky quartz could be a great match for you! Named for its smoky gray color, smoky quartz is both calming and grounding. It can help you to overcome your fears and find balance even when things in your life feel unsteady or even a bit rocky. Place a smoky quartz on your desk or nightstand so you stay centered and calm.

Chapter 8
BIRTH AND DEATH

THIS CHAPTER IS A LIFE-AND-DEATH MATTER—OR AT LEAST, those are the topics of these dreams, and the way they are commonly interpreted. These can be some of the spookiest dreams of all, so tread carefully and don't jump to any assumptions about what they mean and how they apply to your life and your family. Take these with an *extra* grain of salt and keep your sense of humor handy at all times! While they can sometimes be intense, you don't need to let these dreams scare you.

> *fun fact!*
> Most people spend about one-third of their life sleeping.
> That's an average of twenty-six years!

BABIES

Babies are a symbol of innocence, growth, fresh starts, and vulnerability. They are usually a very positive thing to see in a dream, and if one shows up in yours, it might reflect some of those characteristics and how they relate to you. There is something gentle in your soul; you are full of wonder and purity. You see life through childlike eyes. Perhaps your nature is to be trusting and open-minded.

Babies can also reflect new experiences in your life. This dream could be related to a new relationship, a move to another town or school, or something good in your life that you've been waiting for with anticipation. You probably have the opportunity for a fresh start, and this dream is your sign to seize that opportunity. The future is bright, so take the time to give these new things in your life your full attention. Nurture your new experiences.

If the baby in your dream is crying, it's a sign there is something in your life that needs attention. Babies cry when there is something they require, so this baby probably represents an unmet need in your own life. Bring your awareness to the parts of your life you may have been ignoring and give them more of your focus.

DEATH OF A LOVED ONE

Losing someone you care about in a dream can be extremely upsetting. It's the sort of dream that can have you waking up in tears, full of relief to know that you were just sleeping and none of the pain you suffered in your dreams is real. Some people think this dream can be a premonition that someone in the real world is going to pass away, but that is rarely the case. If you take this dream too literally, it can fill you with a lot of unnecessary fear. Death in dreams usually is symbolic of transformation. There might be some big changes going on in your waking life or some aspects of yourself that are being transformed.

This dream is almost always about transition, so be open-minded as you consider its implication for you.

DYING

If you are the person who has died in your dream, there are probably some big changes going on within you. Death in dreams can be tied to change and rebirth. Consider if anything major is happening in your life right now—if you are quitting old habits or developing new ones, if perhaps you've ended an old relationship or struck up a new one.

This dream could also be a sign that you are afraid of the unknown—death signifies something hard to see or uncertain in your future that you don't want to face. Maybe you are about to move to a new town or neighborhood or there's a big decision you need to make soon where you can't know the outcome. Try to remember that the unknown isn't always a bad thing. It can be full of excitement and thrilling new opportunities for you that are just waiting to be uncovered. The way that you die in your dream can give you a hint at what this dream is trying to tell you, too. If it was a scary, violent death, then the dream is more likely to be related to some anxiety in your waking life. If you die a peaceful death, however, it might mean that you are feeling a sense of peace about the changes coming your way.

EXPERIENCING THE END OF THE WORLD

Dreams about the world ending often signify that there are fears and anxieties in your waking life, usually about something in your future. If there are big changes coming your way, this dream can represent your world, as you know it, coming to an end. All things must come to an end eventually, but that doesn't mean it's any less frightening when they do. Though you might be traveling on unfamiliar roads, remember that the ending of one chapter leads to the beginning of another.

Chapter 9
THE BODY

ET'S FACE IT, WE SPEND 24/7/365 INSIDE OUR BODIES, SO IT is only natural that they show up in our dreams. And when they do, it can be in really, really weird ways. There is almost always something kind of wrong going on with your body in the dream, and it can even be comical, so do try to laugh it off when you wake up thinking you can't move your legs or have a chipped tooth. Maybe it is a message, or maybe it is just a strange dream and nothing more. Regardless, perhaps this chapter can give you a bit of insight.

> ### fun fact!
> *Whales and dolphins can only fall half asleep! Because they have to consciously decide to come up to the surface for air, they shut down half of their brains at a time, taking turns between each side while the other half stays awake to breathe and look out for predators. They also only close one eye at a time while they sleep!*

FEET

Feet are grounding, and so they represent stability as well as freedom. Dreams about feet often relate to your sense of practicality and wisdom and can connect to your drive to find success in life. If the dream involves something being wrong with your feet, this might be a sign that you are struggling to find your way in life. You might feel off-balance, like there is something hindering your independence. If the dream was a positive one, this can mean you're feeling confident about where you are in life.

HAIR

Hair in dreams often symbolizes attraction, empowerment, youth, or vanity, and how it looks and feels in your dream reveals your attitude in your waking life. Knotted or tangled hair can relate to feelings of confusion or a series of problems that need to be "untangled." Cutting your hair or getting a new hairstyle represents a major change in your life or a desire to reinvent yourself.

Since hair is related to a sense of self-esteem, losing or damaging your hair can mean that you have experienced a dip in confidence in your waking life. You may be struggling with your body image or feeling anxiety about how you appear to others. Hair loss and baldness in a dream can also be a sign that you are afraid of getting older, and are too focused on your appearance. On the other hand, dreams of long or growing hair can symbolize newfound confidence.

Hair is closely tied to identity in dreams, so think carefully about what you experience in these dreams and how they make you feel.

LOSING YOUR HEAD

Dreaming about being headless is often a sign that there is a disconnect between your head and your heart—what you're thinking and what you're feeling. For example, you might be thinking so much about an upcoming vocabulary test that you lose track of other homework assignments that need to be done because you're so focused on studying. You may be lacking a sense of balance in your life. Try to identify the role that your heart and mind play in your life. Is one taking more control than the other? You may be so intent on common sense and logic that you have started to neglect or suppress your emotions. On the other hand, it's possible that you are letting your feelings dictate your actions without thinking things through.

MISSING A BODY PART

If you find yourself looking down in a dream only to discover that you're suddenly missing an arm, a leg, a finger, etc., that can often be a sign of some kind of loss in your waking life. Whether the dream involves the traumatic loss of a limb or simply its disappearance, the symbolism is deeply tied to feelings of abandonment, helplessness, and sacrifice. This dream can stem from a fear of losing something or someone important to you in real life. The body part likely connects to something you felt was a vital part of yourself that you aren't ready to let go of.

These dreams can, however, also be purifying. The lost limb can be a sign that you need to let go of something that is having a negative effect on your mental health. That thing—be it an extracurricular activity, a relationship, or something else—might play a very important role in your life, which can make the separation harder, but there are sometimes sacrifices that need to happen in order to protect yourself. Specific body parts can also hint at different interpretations. Loss of a leg may be a sign there is something holding you back from following the path you need to take—you are being limited or are struggling to move forward in life. Losing your arm, on the other hand, might indicate that you are feeling a loss of control in your waking life. Try turning this around with some physical movement or exercise you can do. It can be as simple as taking a walk or stretching; even dancing to your favorite song will make you feel better about life in general!

LOSING TEETH

Dental disasters are ranked as one of the most common dreams. Your teeth might crumble to bits in your mouth, rot, or fall out when you bite into something. Most people find these dreams to be quite scary. There are a broad variety of interpretations, so it's important to consider the events and circumstances in your waking life that might apply to these interpretations.

Teeth are a very noticeable physical feature that are often tied to a person's attractiveness, which makes vanity one likely interpretation of this dream. If you're losing your teeth, this can be a sign that you're putting an emphasis on your outward appearance when you think about your value as a person. If you find yourself constantly worried about how other people think you look, remember that attractiveness comes as much from the inside as the outer appearance. It is not just the latest, greatest hairstyle or the fit of your new skinny jeans; your attitude and personality are a big part of your beauty, too!

Losing your teeth can also represent the fear of looking silly or foolish in front of your peers. If you have to give a class presentation or try out for a team or perform in a school play, it's possible that your fear of embarrassing yourself can cause you to dream about missing teeth. More than likely, you have nothing to worry about, and this dream is just a sign that your anxieties have made you start thinking too hard about how others perceive you. Consider who in your life you might be trying to impress and allow yourself the space to make mistakes.

Powerlessness and communication difficulties can be an interpretation of this dream as well. Perhaps you feel like your voice isn't being heard by the people in your life; you might have the impression you don't have the freedom to speak up even when you know something is not right. Don't be afraid to speak your mind and be truthful. Being honest doesn't have to involve acting rude or mean-spirited, either. You can be really nice *and* really candid. What you think matters! So share it.

Sometimes damaged teeth can be a sign of declining health, too. If you haven't been giving your body the care that it needs, this might be an indication to start incorporating better habits into your daily routine. It is important that your body gets enough nutrition, exercise, and sleep!

GETTING SICK

Having dreams about getting sick? Illness in dreams can be related to an illness you or someone in your life is currently experiencing, but it can also show up if you are in an anxious emotional state or experiencing other challenges. Are there any conflicts in your friendships or other relationships? Have you experienced a major change in your life? Do you feel like you're faced with situations you are struggling to cope with or are taking up a lot of your emotional energy? In this case, dreaming about feeling sick could be taken as a sign that you need to better look after your own physical and emotional well-being. On the other hand, it could be a sign that you are trying to avoid your problems rather than facing them head-on.

BLINDNESS

When a seeing person has a dream about becoming blind, it's often a sign that there is something in that person's life they're avoiding or refusing to acknowledge. Maybe you are ghosting a friend because you are annoyed with them about something but don't want or know how to confront them. Perhaps you witnessed something you knew was wrong but did nothing.

Sometimes, when one sense is lost, others are heightened. Blindness may draw your attention to other senses, too, which could mean there is a situation you are involved in that is really about more than what meets the eye. Trust your gut, and don't take everything at face value.

BECOMING INVISIBLE

Invisibility in dreams can reflect feelings of being overlooked in your waking life. If you have dreams in which you're invisible, it likely means you feel that people in your life are not paying attention to you or acknowledging you. Don't be afraid to ask people for what you need.

Becoming invisible in dreams can also be a sign that you are trying to avoid problems in your life—you try to hide as soon as things start to get tough.

Chapter 10
PEOPLE

VERY DAY THE INTERACTIONS WE HAVE WITH PEOPLE IN our lives impact us in some way. We are constantly influenced by our parents, friends, and teachers. We come across so many different people every day that it's hardly surprising they find their way into our dreams, too! Human beings are meant to live together in harmony and community, where we can learn from each other and share in joy and acceptance.

If you are dreaming of a parent or parental figure that does not fit into the two categories of mother and father, or who uses one of these labels but does not fit the traditional categorical description for either, your interpretation will mostly be guided by the role they play in your life, in the family dynamic, and your personal associations with them. In the same way, the people we spend time with inside our dreams might

fun fact!

While dreams can happen at any time during our sleep, most of them occur during the REM stage. These dreams are usually the strangest—but also the most vivid ones in our sleep cycle. This stage is the part of the sleep cycle when our brains are the most active.

appear as a gift from our subconscious, ready to impart life lessons and important revelations about our own selves. Keep an open heart and mind as you listen to what they might be trying to tell you.

FAMILY MEMBERS

Dreams about your family often symbolize some aspect of your relationship with them. They can be related to specific things that happened, or they reflect your overall bond with that person. Family can often be a symbol of comfort and security, particularly if you feel like you have a good relationship with them. If you are seeing family members that you have a messy relationship with, this could reflect feelings of bitterness, turmoil, rivalry, and other negative emotions. It all depends on what associations you have with those people in your real life.

Mothers

If your mother is making an appearance in your dream, she likely is acting as a symbol of some of the things that we usually associate with mother figures: warmth, tenderness, and nurturing. The symbolic role of the mother in your dream can vary, however, depending on your family's dynamic. If the mom in your dream has, say, superpowers, it might be a sign that a woman you know can help you in real life. Maybe it is a female teacher, an older sister, or your own mom!

Fathers

Parental figures often symbolize knowledge, authority, discipline, and finance. These features are, of course, very subjective and will be different depending on your own idea of what a parent should be, since these associations with family members have historically been connected to gender roles in the family unit. If you have a dream in which your father is on a team you are playing against, it could be a sign that you need to improve your communication with him. Maybe just talk to him or hang out and simply spend time together; that way, you can get on the same team in real life! Your father can represent some of the ideas tied to the role he plays in your family or specific parts of your relationship with him. The dream may be showing you there are parts of his character that you wish to or should try to embody in your waking life. Are there parts of his character that you really admire and would like to show more of yourself?

Grandparents

To see either or both of your grandparents in your dream can often be a reflection of wisdom and protection or of the traditions, values, and morals that were passed down to you. Their appearance may be a sign to draw from the collective wisdom of your elders, but it could also indicate that it is time to evaluate the beliefs you have inherited from generations past and decide which are genuinely valuable today and which have become outdated and need to be left in the past. Grandparents are very commonly associated with caring, so in that case you might be experiencing a longing to be cared for.

Siblings

When siblings appear in your dream, they can direct your attention to your own role in the family or mirror parts of your personality. Look for traits in your sibling that you see in yourself—this dream can be a sign to get in touch with those parts of yourself on a deeper level. Some other associations related to siblings are rivalry, friendship, and comradery. Your waking relationship with the sibling you see and the feelings you experience toward them during the dream will help guide your interpretations.

MEETING A CELEBRITY

A celebrity encounter can often be a very exciting dream to have, as it's often wrapped up in feelings of admiration—especially if it's a celebrity that you are a big fan of in your waking life. If this is the case, it is possible the dream is the result of your desire to meet that celebrity in real life. Then, this dream can become a form of wish fulfillment. It's common to dream about celebrity crushes if your waking thoughts are filled with them.

However, a common interpretation of this sort of dream is also that the celebrity represents specific qualities you want to grow in yourself. Think about the celebrity that you met in your dream and what traits you associate with them. Are you in awe of their charisma, activism, or specific talent? What is that celebrity known for? Do you idolize that celebrity, and if so, why? Think about how you might relate to any aspects of that celebrity's stage personality or career, since that is what will guide your interpretation. This dream may be encouraging you to think about how you can better represent the traits you admire in others.

MEETING A STRANGER

The strangers we see in our dreams often embody hidden parts of our own selves. A stranger is a symbol of something that has been repressed or is unknown to us right now, and by recognizing these parts of us when they appear in our dreams, we can learn more about ourselves. Think about the strangers you meet and interact with in your dreams and how they make you feel. Are they frightening? Friendly? What is it about them that makes you feel that way? Often some of the observations you make about these strangers are connected to your personality, and how they make you feel can have something to do with your reaction to those parts of yourself. How you interact with them can indicate whether you have accepted these things or are denying/avoiding them. The most important thing to remember is that they are there to teach us if we are willing to be open to what they represent.

SEEING AN OLD FRIEND

When you see an old friend in your dream, it can be a sign of emotions from your past resurfacing or circumstances and people in your current life that remind you of someone from your past. These dreams often feel nostalgic. Perhaps you are missing something from that time in your life or have some unfinished business with your old friend or with that past version of yourself. Usually, these dreams are not about that particular old friend, but connect to something or someone in your current waking life. There might be aspects of that person's personality that can give you some insight into some of the ways you are dealing with everyday stress, or you could have something to learn from your memories of them. When a friend you had a falling out with shows up in your dreams, it can often mean that you have some leftover feelings of guilt and loss.

Dreaming about an old friend is not necessarily a sign that you should reconnect with them—whether they belong in your current life or not is personal to you, and should be considered with caution, especially if that friend was one who hurt you. It may be time to forge some new connections—part of you is missing the feeling of having a relationship like the one you had with your old friend.

A TEACHER

Teachers act as a symbol of knowledge. Dreaming about a teacher from either your past or present likely means that you are seeking answers or guidance in your life. They might represent the solution to a current dilemma you're facing or simply your desire for knowledge and wisdom. Teachers act as authority figures, so you might be wanting advice, instruction, or approval from someone you look up to.

Think about your relationship with the teacher that appeared in your dream and how that relationship might inform your understanding of what you have left to learn. A particularly stern teacher might symbolize some part of your life in which you are feeling scrutinized. Sometimes a dream about a teacher can reflect some changes or new experiences in life that are leaving you feeling a bit lost. Learning from your past experiences may help you navigate this new path.

AN UNINVITED GUEST

If you have a dream about an unexpected or uninvited guest, your reaction to that person can be a good indicator of how you should interpret the dream. A pleasant visit can be a good sign. For example, someone comes knocking at your door and you are filled with excitement and invite them in—the experience is more a pleasant surprise than a disruption. This shows that you are adaptable and open to sudden changes. When something unexpected comes up in your waking life, you take it in stride and are able to be flexible and accommodating. If the surprise visit makes you feel anxious or scared, or the visitor is someone you dislike, this might reflect that you feel your privacy has been violated in some way in your real life. There may be people that are prying too deeply into your personal life or intruding on you constantly. In this case, this dream may be calling attention to that and can be taken as an encouragement to create more healthy boundaries.

Chapter 11
PLACES

WE OFTEN DREAM ABOUT REAL-LIFE PLACES—ANY-where from spots we'd like to go to ones we visit all the time, like school and home. Your dreams recreate worlds based on experiences and knowledge that you carry with you in your waking life, often using familiar things that might even make a place of comfort for you in the dream realm. Don't be surprised if you find your-self replicating various locations from your memories. It is said that the places you visit in your dreams can also represent states of mind. What could some of these dreams say about you?

>*fun fact!*
>
>After the age of ten, we have at least
>four to six dreams a night.

SCHOOL

Even now, I have dreams of forgetting to study for a test or showing up at school unprepared in some way with no books or bag, pencils or notebooks. Our school years are such important experiences in our lives. From classrooms to band practice to hallways filled with lockers, school buildings are hard coded in our brains, and the pressure(s) you feel as a student can pop up when you least expect it. A very commonplace dream is about not finishing school or having to repeat a year. These dreams can be little nudges to pay attention to deadlines and priorities. They can also be a sign that you need to decompress and do something fun and relaxing to let go of worries. Take a run, shoot some hoops on the court, meet up with friends, or whatever else will help you clear your mind!

YOUR HOME

Having a dream about your house is usually a sign that part of you wants to revisit the past. Think about how your home makes you feel and how it appears in the dream. Is it a comforting place? If so, perhaps you are looking for a sense of comfort and security that is missing from your real life right now. If there's something uneasy about your dream, it's possible that you need to do something to make yourself more comfortable. Perhaps you can give your bedroom a simple makeover with a new comforter, throw pillows, and a cool new lamp. Make your space your personal sanctuary and a place where you can relax and feel good. After all, your bedroom is a real center of activity where you do homework, read, sleep, hang out with friends, and relax. Make sure you feel really happy in your room and your life will be happier too!

AN ATTIC

Attics symbolize the higher, spiritual self. If you're having a dream about an attic, or one that takes place in an attic, your dream is probably trying to tell you something about your spiritual life and well-being. Notice the state of the attic and your feelings toward it. Attics can also be related to memories and hidden or repressed thoughts. Is the attic scary? Is it dark? A cluttered attic can be related to a cluttered mind, meaning you might need to work on organizing your thoughts in your waking life. You might be putting too many things on your plate—a sign you might need to sort out your priorities. A dark attic could mean there are some parts of your-self you aren't ready to face or that you're dealing with a lot of uncer-tainty in your spiritual life. A clean or bright attic, on the other hand, would be a positive sign that your mind is clear and you are open to the world around you. Use context to help you interpret what this dream has to say about your memories, emotions, and spirituality.

A BASEMENT

Basements usually represent some part of your subconscious; they can symbolize some of your deepest thoughts and emotions. A dark base-ment might be a sign that there is some uncertainty in your life. If the dark basement in your dream feels frightening, it is possible that you're worried about certain aspects of your personality and allowing yourself to be vulnerable. A musty old basement might mean some part of your life feels stale, or that you've lost your motivation. The basement in your dream is trying to bring something that has been lingering in your sub-conscious mind into your awareness, so pay close attention to whatever details you can remember from the dream. Are there unexpected objects in the basement? While these dreams can seem scary at first, they serve as reminders that we cannot control every aspect of life, so try to go with the flow and release whatever might be causing your anxiety.

DISCOVERING A SECRET ROOM

Dreaming about discovering secret rooms is a metaphor for discovering new things about yourself in your waking life. This may be an invitation for you to explore parts of yourself that perhaps you didn't know existed before—some personality traits, desires, various aspects of your identity, etc. The dream may be drawing your attention to a part of you that you've forgotten or neglected, especially if the room you find looks dusty or empty. Maybe you have a hidden talent you need to tap into, such as taking up a musical instrument, drawing, or playing a sport. Open the door to this previously unknown part of you! Finding secret rooms can also be a symbol for new experiences or people that have come into your waking life. There is a world of possibility in your life waiting to be explored if you have the courage to step inside those mysterious rooms and open up to new things!

A PASSAGEWAY

Passageways can appear in our dreams in various ways—as a brightly lit hall, a dark corridor, a cave route with a light shining at the other end, and so on. These dreams are usually a sign that you're experiencing a transition in your waking life. You might be feeling some changes in your beliefs or opinions, transferring schools, starting up a new hobby, or making new friends. The passage is often connected to a general sense of something unexpected and thrilling that is occurring in your waking life. If the passage seems dark and scary in the dream, it might be a sign that you're feeling nervous about these changes and what lies on the other side, while a light at the end of the tunnel could mean you are remaining hopeful in the midst of that uncertainty. Proceed with caution, if necessary, but try to be optimistic and trust yourself to navigate through these unfamiliar circumstances.

A GARDEN

Gardens take a lot of time and care to maintain, so having a dream about a garden is often symbolic of productivity, nurturing, and personal growth. Try to recall what the garden in your dreams looked like. Was it healthy and full of flowers? Was it overgrown or dried out? A messy garden can be a sign that you are neglecting yourself and your needs. You might not be putting in the necessary effort to accomplish your goals. Take this as a sign to roll up your sleeves and focus on looking after yourself and finding activities or people that bring you joy. If you are dreaming of a garden full of fruits and vegetables, this dream might be a sign that you want to build a healthier lifestyle for yourself.

A beautiful, blooming garden is probably a positive sign that you are doing well and are giving proper care and attention to all of the things that matter most in your life, and it may also be showing you your potential—what you could become if you take the time to nurture your symbolic garden. Perhaps it's time to strengthen the relationships in your waking life. It will take time and effort to see growth, whether that is related to inner nurturing, a relationship, a new hobby you are learning, better grades in school, or something else entirely. Whatever it is for you, if you tend to it diligently, the fruit of your efforts will be amazing.

A DEEP FOREST

Trees are symbolic of life, hope, wisdom, and growth, so when you see a forest in your dreams, that can have a lot of similar meanings. Having a dream about walking through a forest can be a sign that you're in a transitional phase of life, full of new growth and opportunities. You can gain a lot of knowledge from listening to and learning from the people surrounding you. Forests can also represent your subconscious, taking you on a journey through your own mind to learn more about yourself. You might be starting to become more aware of your own potential—the height of the trees showing you how far up you can reach and the size reminding you of your own inner strength. Venturing into a forest can signify your desire to get more in touch with nature and find quiet in today's active and busy culture. Open yourself up to the wonder that surrounds you.

ROADS

Unsurprisingly, roads in your dreams usually have a meaning related to your direction and goals in life. The appearance of the road will usually say something about how your journey is going and what kind of obstacles you are facing. A straight, clear path is probably a sign that things have been going well in your life and you have a good sense of where you are heading and how you are getting there. Keep on going and trust that your efforts will pay off. On the other hand, the road in your dream could also have been a twisty, winding route with bumps and potholes along the way. It's possible that you're having a dream like this because you've been dealing with a lot of challenges. Maybe you don't have a clear idea of what you want in your life, or you have a goal but haven't established a clear path to reach it. If this feels accurate, you might need to take some time to slow down and think about how best to move forward. Talk to someone you trust—a friend or teacher or grown-up—that can help you figure out a plan.

PRISON

Having a dream about being in prison probably means that you're feeling restricted in some part of your waking life. Maybe there is a situation that you can't get out of no matter how badly you want to escape. Maybe you really don't like your first class in the morning and feel a sense of dread. Accepting that you can't just stop going to class and, instead, trying to find the positive—maybe you have a friend in the class or maybe your favorite class will be right after—can help. Shifting the focus even a little can make a huge difference. You'll be amazed at what happens!

Jail is also associated with censorship, so you might be feeling like you can't speak your mind. This dream may be a sign that it's time to draw some boundaries—it's OK to say no to hanging out with people or doing things that don't interest you. Reclaim your voice and don't be afraid of saying what's in your heart.

WAYS TO PRACTICE SELF-CARE
ACCORDING TO YOUR DREAM LIFE

Choose the answer that best suits you for
each of these open-ended phrases.

A dream that would be most exciting to have is . . .

A. Getting a great gift from someone you care about

B. Going on vacation

C. Having a bubble tea outing with friends

The animals I like most are . . .

A. Dogs

B. Birds

C. Cats

A dream I would least like to have is . . .

A. Being lied to

B. Being trapped

C. Going into a dark, creepy basement

The symbol I see in my dreams most often is . . .

A. A garden

B. An airplane

C. The ocean

IF YOU ANSWERED MOSTLY A'S . . . You're someone who really values your relationships with others. You put a lot of time and effort into growing and nurturing those connections. You trust and admire all of the people you bring into your life, and you're the most dedicated, loyal friend anyone could ask for. When you're feeling down, a phone call with a friend or relative that you haven't talked to in a while might be just the thing you need. If you need a little more face-to-face connection, invite a friend over for some fun!

IF YOU ANSWERED MOSTLY B'S . . . You are an independent thinker, full of ambition. You probably don't like to be tied down or stuck at home for too long, and you're the sort of person who finds adventure everywhere. Take care of yourself by making the time to go out and do something that makes you happy. Take a walk, go on a hike, visit a park, or go for a bike ride. Use the outdoors as a release for your stress. If all the hard work you've been putting into chasing after your goals has you feeling exhausted, another great way to look after yourself is to create a relaxing experience at home by taking a nice, long bubble bath or curling up with your favorite book in your favorite chair.

IF YOU ANSWERED MOSTLY C'S . . . You're probably in a phase of life where you're exploring new things and getting to know yourself better. You might also be trying to understand parts of yourself that aren't so pretty or feelings you don't like having to confront. A great way to practice self-care during this period of self-discovery is to keep a journal. This will help you organize and process all your thoughts and feelings. Practice self-love by jotting down a list of at least five things that you like about yourself.

Chapter 12
COMMUNICATION

C OMMUNICATION IS SUCH AN IMPORTANT PART OF OUR lives. It's necessary not only in the practical sense, but also for our sense of empathy. It's important that we stay in touch and in tune with the people who are important to us as well as with our inner selves. In an age when technology sometimes seems to create more over-stimulation but also keeps us at a distance from the on-screen action, it can get harder and harder to find that connection. All these dreams are commonly interpreted as having something to do with the ways we are communicating in our waking lives, so think about whether any of these interpretations might apply to you. Maybe they can even encourage you to become a better listener or work on how you convey your feelings to others.

⊷— ❧ *fun fact!* ❧ —⊶

Some people can learn to have lucid dreams! Lucid dreaming is when a person becomes aware that they are dreaming and can control the things that happen in their dreams—meaning they can go anywhere or do anything they can possibly imagine!

PHONES

Phones are the main way we communicate. We rely so much on our cell phones to stay in touch with our friends, family, and the events happening in the world around us. Because of that, when we see a phone in our dreams, the condition the phone is in can give us some insight into the ways we are connecting in our waking life. If there is a specific person you are calling or trying to call in your dream, then you can look at the telephone as a representation of the link between that person and yourself. There might be a circumstance in your life where you are looking for connection and need to be the one to reach out.

Your Cell Phone Is Cracked

Since phones are a symbol of communication, cracking your cell phone in a dream is generally associated with a relationship that has been damaged. It can often be a sign there is a friendship in your life that feels beyond repair or a connection between you and someone in your life that used to come easy but now requires extra effort to maintain. Somewhere in your waking life, you are likely feeling that there are some broken lines of communication.

If, in the dream, you have broken your phone on purpose, that could mean you are craving distance from a relationship in your life. It represents your desire to cut ties with someone, so if you are involved with someone who is bringing negativity or drama into your life, your subconscious might be telling you it's time to let go of that relationship.

Your Phone Isn't Working

If you are trying to reach someone in your dream and the call just won't go through—perhaps the call is breaking up, you get disconnected every time you try to call, or you get sent to voicemail—it's probably a sign that you are feeling distant or cut off from someone you care about. There may be a person in your life who is not being open to your attempts to communicate with them. You are trying to express your needs or feelings about something but are not being heard. Do you find that in your waking life you feel the efforts you are putting into a relationship aren't being reciprocated? Try to see if there is a need in your life that is not being met, or if there is a situation where you need to express yourself more confidently to be heard. If you can identify a relationship that is growing distant, this dream may be your sign to reach out to that person and reestablish a line of communication.

YOU'RE UNABLE TO SPEAK

This is another dream that's related to your ability to communicate. Often in these dreams, you are trying to scream or shout for help, but every time you do, no sound comes out. It can be a very frightening

dream, connected to feelings of terror or extreme anxiety. When you find yourself unable to open your mouth or speak in a dream, it's a sign that something has gone wrong in your waking life. You may be feeling like you aren't being heard or that you are struggling to express yourself.

It could also be a sign that you are feeling helpless. You might want help from someone in your life, but your own feelings of pride or uncertainty are holding you back from getting the assistance you need. Or perhaps you *have* initiated that call for help, but you feel like your concerns aren't being heard or valued. Try to think about what situations might be causing you to feel ignored. It's likely a need for some form of acknowledgment that is causing this dream.

HAVING GLASS IN YOUR MOUTH

Dreaming about chewing or suddenly having shards of broken glass in your mouth is often a sign that you are struggling to say what needs to be said in real life because you're afraid of what will happen next. Another interpretation is that you are having a difficult time expressing your needs or are too proud to open up to others and show your vulnerable side—or perhaps you feel like you *can't* express that side of yourself. It's also possible this dream is a warning from your subconscious that you need to watch your mouth. There are, after all, times when it's best to keep your opinions to yourself. In this case, the glass pieces in your mouth might symbolize the damaging power that your words can have for the people in your life.

Chapter 13
MOVEMENT DREAMS

LOOK FORWARD TO FLYING DREAMS—I FEEL SO EMPOWERED BY them! I feel like a superhero who can go anywhere I want. I am sure you have similar dreams and enjoy the sensation of being like a bird or even a supernatural being as you swoop around the sky. Dreams like these, as well as other movement-related dreams, can give you very important clues about your own personal power. Enjoy!

CLIMBING

An uphill climb is usually related to some kind of struggle in your waking life. This dream could involve a hill, a mountain, a ladder, etc. How steep the climb is and how much difficulty you have making it can be a reflection of similar circumstances in your waking life. If the climb is really hard, it could be that the obstacle you are facing or the thing you hope to achieve is turning out to be more than you bargained for. You might be trying to grow your circle of friends, join a team or club, or reach some other new goal. If it feels like things are going too slowly, maybe you need to step back and evaluate the situation and come up with a better path to get you to where you want to be. Success is in your future if you approach it the right way.

DANCING

Dance is a way to express yourself that, in our dreams, can symbolize freedom, joy, and passion. If you're dancing in your dream, your subconscious might be encouraging you to set yourself free and relax. Think about your waking life and what sort of situations might be putting pressure on you. If you feel like your individuality is being stifled or you are overwhelmed with too many obligations like school activities, work, clubs, etc., this dream might be your subconscious telling you to live a little. It's OK to let go and let loose. Let your creativity flow—you will start to feel much happier once you do!

MOVING IN SLOW MOTION

Dreams about moving in slow motion can be taken as a sign to slow down in your waking life. You might be rushing into new relationships, experiences, or responsibilities without allowing time to process what is already around you. Pay attention to the people, places, and things in your waking life. Work on increasing your mindfulness and appreciating what you already have before you start seeking out more. You probably need to focus on taking life one step at a time—otherwise, one day, you'll regret the things you missed in the moment they were happening. These dreams can also draw your attention to overlooked details. When you are moving in slow motion, you might notice things you never would have if you were going at a regular pace. Pay attention to the details and hints in your waking life that you would normally gloss over. There might be something for you to learn there.

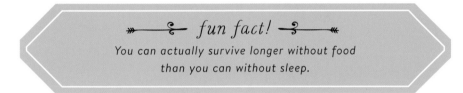

fun fact!
You can actually survive longer without food
than you can without sleep.

RUNNING IN PLACE

Having a dream about running in place—being unable to get anywhere no matter how fast you go—probably means that you are stuck in the past. Something has happened in your life that you are unable to move on from, and this dream is bringing your attention to it. Because you are not totally present in your waking life, you are missing opportunities for growth that will be necessary as you grow up. In this case, the inability to make progress might represent your own stubbornness and dislike for change.

JUMPING

This dream can be interpreted several ways—it all depends on the situation and how the dream made you feel. Dreams about suddenly being able to jump really high can be exhilarating, but they can also feel scary.

Jumping up high can mean falling very far at the same time, so if you jumped up in the air and were filled with sudden terror as you started to fall back down, this dream might mean you've set your goals really high and are afraid of letting people down. It can also mean you're not able to handle the pressure you've put on yourself. On the other hand, if you are enjoying yourself in the dream, it means you're taking the difficult things life throws at you in stride. Dreaming about jumping high can also be a symbol of newfound freedom or the relief that comes along with letting go of something that has been stressing you out. Maybe you've quit a bad habit like biting your nails, eating too much candy and sweets, or you've ended a toxic friendship. Whatever it is, you're starting fresh. If you are feeling bogged down in life, you can take this dream as a sign that you can and should try to release some of the things dragging you down so you can live in a more lighthearted, carefree way.

FLYING

Flying is one of the most common dreams, not to mention one of the most fun! If you're soaring through the air in your dream, gazing out over the earth beneath you, you are probably feeling on top of the world in your waking life. Flight represents freedom and release, so this dream might be a sign that you are experiencing some of those feelings in your life, or it could be encouragement to let loose. Dreams of flying suggest that you have confidence in your ability to rise above challenges that come your way. You can do anything or be anything your heart desires—there are no limits to what you can do.

Another way to interpret this dream is that it's time to broaden your perspectives. When you are flying, you see the world from a completely different view. There are things you might notice that you didn't before,

or you might learn about things in ways you didn't know were possible: seeing how the rivers connect to each other or the details of the trees. This bird's-eye view offers a reminder to take a step back and look at your life in a new way. Maybe you need to be more open-minded about the opinions of those around you or develop a better understanding of how your actions influence the people in your life.

WALKING

Dreams about walking often symbolize patience. When we walk some-where, instead of running or driving in a car, we have much more time to take in our surroundings. Walking is a sign that you aren't in a rush or feeling pressured to get somewhere at a specific time. Step by step, you move forward, absorbing everything around you. If you apply this idea to your waking life, you might take it as a sign that you're taking your time in life, little by little getting to where you need to be, whether that is in terms of achievement, self-fulfillment, or spirituality. You're making consistent progress without feeling like you have to rush and play catch-up. Bring your attention to your surroundings in your dream, your destination, or any other details like obstacles that might better help you form your interpretation.

AIRPLANES

Airplanes are dream symbols often associated with journeys—sometimes spiritual, emotional, or literal. An airplane appearing in your dream can be a sign that you are progressing or moving up in some area of your life. It might also be a sign that it's time to get a new project "off the ground." If you've been sitting on any big plans for your future, perhaps it's time to start putting them into action. This dream can also be about exploring your freedom and trying out new experiences. Pay attention to the state of the plane and how it could relate to events in your life. If the plane is delayed or stuck, it might mean there is something you've been looking forward to that hasn't become a reality yet or some plans that have been put off. It may be that you are afraid to take the next steps to follow through with those plans.

If you're in a plane crash in your dream, that might represent a failed project or something you were looking forward to that didn't work out in the end. It can also be a sign that although you have set high goals for yourself, you are afraid that your efforts will result in failure. Like falling dreams, this can also be a sign that you feel like you are losing control.

BOATS

Having dreams about boats is often a sign of how well you are navigating your emotions in your waking life. How do you cope when bad situations come your way—do you sink into a sea of negative emotions, or do you stay afloat through the storm? Try to remember what the water looked like in your dream. Were there calm waters and clear skies? This could mean that you are experiencing "smooth sailing" in your life. You confidently handle your own emotions and everything in your life feels like it's under control. On the other hand, if the boat experienced rough seas in your dream—crashing waves or winds tearing at the sails—it might mean that you're struggling to keep your emotions under control. You might be feeling overwhelmed in your waking life or letting unhappy thoughts and feelings get the better of you. Think about ways that you can comfortably and safely express what you are feeling. Let this negativity run its course, but don't let it sink you.

CARS

Cars are symbolic of control, ambition, and progress in life. Dreams about cars often signify something about how you are getting on in life and the direction you are taking your future. Cars are a tool we use to get from one place to another, so this dream might be about how you are moving between phases of life, how fast or slow you are progressing, and what sort of obstacles you have experienced or are currently experiencing in your journey to become a more mature and wiser person. If you are riding in a car, that can say something about the role you are playing in your own destiny. Being the driver can be a sign you have taken charge of your own life, while being a passenger might mean that you play a passive role in your life and let other people make the big decisions for you— although your mind might not have a firm idea to share in your dreams of what driving feels like before you are sixteen and fully licensed!

Chapter 14
NATURE AND
NATURAL DISASTERS

←→⦿←→

THESE DREAMS CAN RANGE FROM PEACEFUL AND CALMING to absolutely terrifying, but that's the natural world, isn't it? The ocean can be gentle and beautiful one moment, but also violent and dangerous another time. Dreams about nature can have a lot of different meanings, especially when we look at the various elements that show up. But whether you're dreaming about, say, a lovely snow day versus getting caught in an avalanche, recognize the dream for what it is and don't give it the power to frighten you. Maybe Mother Nature has something to teach you. Meditate on it, learn what you can from it, and then let it pass. (See page 20 on how to meditate.)

TORNADO

While the first thing that comes to mind when you think of tornadoes might be *The Wizard of Oz,* this dream probably isn't about a magical getaway over a rainbow. The violent, swirling winds of a tornado are usually connected to strong negative emotions like anxiety, anger, and despair. Tornadoes are a very volatile natural phenomenon—they appear and disappear suddenly. Even though they are short-lived, they can cause a lot of damage in a brief amount of time. The tornado might be a reflection of your mental state or the emotional state of somebody else in your life.

Have you been feeling prone to mood swings or sudden bouts of over-whelming emotion? This dream might be drawing your attention to that and to the harm your behavior has caused or could cause people in your life. It could also be a sign there are some destructive people in your life that you need to distance yourself from before you get swept up into their drama. Try to identify things in your life that are making you feel overwhelmed and think about ways to calm the storm. There might be something that's making you feel like you're spinning out of control, but keep heart—it will not last long and the sun *will* come out again.

MOUNTAINS

Mountains serve as a symbol of some sort of challenge or obstacle. Seeing mountains in your dream is probably a sign there is something in your waking life that you must overcome—or perhaps you already have. A mountain represents hard work and persistence, encouraging the dreamer to continue striving toward their goals and not to back down even if the path forward looks like a difficult one. Whatever is at the top of *your* mountain, don't be afraid to put in the effort it takes to make it up there! The mountaintop may represent a goal, spiritual growth, enlightenment, or new knowledge. Whatever it means to you, take this dream as a sign to be ambitious and to persevere through any challenges that lie ahead of you.

AN EXPLOSION

The most common interpretation of seeing or experiencing an explosion in your dreams is repression. The explosion may be your mind's way of expressing feelings that have been welling up inside you, just waiting to burst. You may have been holding back certain emotions and, in doing so, only aggravated them in the long term. Anger is the emotion most commonly associated with explosions, so this dream may be a sign that you need to work through some anger issues in your waking life. Perhaps you've been holding in your anger toward someone, and because you've been tucking it away so long, that anger has transformed into a deeply harbored resentment for that person. It's also possible there is a situation that has been gradually escalating in your waking life. It might have the potential to become explosive, so this dream may be a sign to work on de-escalating or distancing yourself from this situation for your own safety.

FIRE

Fire can be a powerful dream symbol. It is the element of both light and life *and* destruction. Fire breathes, it creates energy, and it can be a great tool—but when used carelessly, it destroys everything in its path. It can represent passion, purity, and insight, as well as ruin. Consider some of the ways you could apply this symbol to your waking life. Make sure that you can manage the things you already have on your plate before taking on a new responsibility. Then again, perhaps you are living your life in a way that is making you feel energized. If so, keep it up!

Think about what the fire in your dreamscape looks like. Is it contained, or is it a raging blaze, consuming everything in its wake? An out-of-control fire can represent something that is getting out of control in your waking life, while a calm, controlled fire can be a sign that things are going well for you. The fire could be symbolic of your own warmth and generosity. Fire also illuminates, so it can be interpreted as something that has come to light in your waking life, giving you a better perspective. Notice the emotions you were experiencing: Fear? Apathy? Delight? Were you running from the fire or trapped in it? Did you tend it, putting your utmost care into nurturing it and helping it grow? Your feelings toward the fire will be important in your interpretation, too.

WATER

Water is the element of emotion. Dreams about water generally relate to the thoughts and emotions of your subconscious mind—think of what's "beneath the surface." Water can symbolize life and rebirth, depth, healing, and spirituality. Looking at the state of the water as it appears in your dream can say a lot about yourself and what dwells beneath your emotional surface. Even a placid lake is teeming with life, color, and movement when you dive in. Rough waters could be a sign of emotional turmoil or a general state of distress, while murky waters can mean that your mind is clouded or there are negative thoughts and feelings hindering your spiritual life and emotional health. They can also symbolize a need for some change in your waking life.

THE OCEAN

The appearance of an ocean in your dreams has the same significance that water as a whole does, but the ocean's expansiveness can also have some implications for your waking life. The ocean is powerful, it has untold depths yet to be explored and horizons that seem infinite. Its vastness can represent possibility and wonder in your waking life—the horizons of what you can become and what you are capable of are wider than the eye can see. Perhaps there are depths to your personality that you should be exploring as well, hidden parts of yourself that deserve to be brought into the light and a complexity of emotions that you have yet to address. You are an intricate, powerful being.

A RIVER

Rivers often serve as a symbol of change, journey, and direction. We know that rivers are in constant motion, traveling from one place to another. The dream river likely has something to reveal to you about your life journey and the direction your future is going. A calm river can be a sign that you are going with the flow, letting life's currents carry you wherever they lead. Trust that you will end up where you need to be and don't be afraid to go at your own pace, taking things one day at a time. A rushing river might be a sign you're getting swept up in your own emotions or that you are moving too fast in some area of your waking life with nothing to steady yourself or hold on to. You might not like the direction your life is going but feel powerless to change its course. The river can symbolize big changes coming your way and opportunities to alter your perspectives. The symbolic cleansing powers of the river can indicate that it's time to let go of the old and open yourself up to the new.

fun fact!

We can't read, write, or tell the time
when we are dreaming.

RAIN

Rain is generally seen as a metaphor for tears, so dreaming of rain might be a sign that there is some deep sadness in your waking life. Something might be weighing heavily on your heart that needs a release—perhaps you have been holding a lot of emotions in and, like the rain falling out of the sky, you need to let those feelings out in order for you to move on and begin to heal. Is there a friend or family member with whom you've had a fight? Talking through what happened can help. Or maybe you are just feeling sad or "off"—we all have those moments. Don't be afraid to reach out to someone to talk about how you're feeling. Rain can also serve as a symbol of healing, washing away past pain and hurt feelings that you've been carrying around. It may be time to forgive yourself or someone in your life and let feelings of resentment or guilt wash off you. This dream is encouragement to make way for a fresh, clear sky.

A MASSIVE WAVE

Dreaming about a giant wave, like a tidal wave or tsunami, is also usually connected to your emotions. So a dream about waves, especially a huge, intimidating one, probably says something about how you are feeling in your daily life. You may be experiencing a lot of pressure to live up to someone else's expectations, or you may just be holding on to a lot of strong emotions. These feelings have probably been building up inside you for a while, which is why they are culminating in one big wave. Your feelings must be confronted soon, or else you might reach a point when they come pouring out all at once whether you like it or not.

QUICKSAND

Quicksand is likely something few of us have ever actually encountered, but we've all seen it in enough movies to understand the danger it poses.

Having a dream of quicksand is likely a sign that you need some stability. The quicksand represents something that is making you feel stuck, trapped in place with nowhere to run. Consider what in your life could be holding you back from reaching your full potential. Take time in your real life to slow down and give attention to the things that might be causing you to feel this way, so you can figure out a solution. Maybe you feel stuck on a school project or practicing your musical instrument seems very repetitive. These kinds of dreams serve as reminders to stay on a clear path and keep going to the next destination or phase.

A RAINBOW

Rainbows are a positive dream symbol that many think is a sign of good luck and fortune—good things are ahead in your future. We can also look at rainbows as a sign of hope. Just like rainbows appear after a heavy rain, this dream may be a sign to hold out through tough times and trust there is good that will come out of your difficulties once they have passed. Rainbows are also considered to be a bridge, connecting your physical self with your spiritual self. In this case, your dream may be calling attention to an imbalance between these two sides of yourself. For example, maybe you have been focusing on an upcoming event—school dance, homecoming, talent show, birthday party, etc.—and have been preoccupied with shopping, picking the right outfit, and getting ready. Take a breath and take it easy and take a more relaxed approach.

You'll end up having more fun, too!

Chapter 15
THE ANIMAL KINGDOM

←——— ⊕ ———→

LIONS AND TIGERS AND BEARS, OH MY! I COULD WRITE A whole book just about animal dreams and their meanings! Animals are often seen as spiritual guides in dreams and have symbolic significance in cultures all around the world. And while dreaming about a lovable furry or scaly companion can of course be about a pet from your waking life, there is also a possibility that they are in your dream life to offer you some guidance or wisdom.

Dreaming about animals can reflect something about your instinctual nature, your hidden desires, or some unknown/unexplored parts of your personality. It might be time to connect with your wild side or release some of your inhibitions and live more freely. Think about the animals that appear in your dream: what sort of traits do you associate with them, and how did you interact with those animals? Did you care for them? Did you befriend them? Were you running from or attacked by them?

CATS

Cats are a dream symbol that is usually related to concepts like curiosity, femininity, and independence. Your personal feelings toward cats will be the driving force in your interpretation, but you might find that this dream is related to you getting in touch with some of those specific things in your waking life. This dream might be encouraging you to be curious and approach life with a sense of wonder. Perhaps you have been trying to engage with your feminine side on a deeper level. Or maybe you have been relying on others too much, and the appearance of a cat in your dream is your unconscious's way of letting you know that it's OK to take control of your own life. You are the designer of your destiny, and you won't be able to reach your full potential if you are using the people in your life as a crutch. This dream might also just be a sign for you to be quiet and attentive in your waking life, waiting patiently for the right moment to pounce on a new opportunity.

> ⤏ ⸜ *fun fact!* ⸝ ⤎
>
> *People aren't the only ones that dream! Animals seem to experience the same sleep stages that humans do, and research shows that it is very likely that our pets have complex dreams, just like us.*

DOGS

It's no surprise that dogs can be very meaningful symbols in our dreams. More than anything, we associate dogs with loyalty. We've all grown up hearing stories about dogs who protect and watch over their owners, assist in daring rescues, and even detect illness in their family. Service dogs can be life-changing companions for people with disabilities. Likewise, as a dream symbol, dogs can represent loyalty, protection, innocence, and companionship. This dream might relate to how those traits are reflected in yourself, or they could be related to another person in your life that is full of some of that doglike spirit. The events of your dream could also be related to the friendships in your life and to your own sense of security. Perhaps dreaming about dogs is a sign for you to embrace life with a puppylike innocence and sincerity.

If the dream is a negative one, however—perhaps involving some-thing like a dog attack—it might symbolize betrayal. Because dogs are loved for their loyalty, when you have a dream of getting bitten or attacked by a dog, that is a betrayal of all they represent to us. This dream could accompany events in your waking life where you felt betrayed by someone you trusted. Or perhaps you yourself wronged someone who trusted you. In this situation, the aggressive dog might represent you and is drawing attention to your own mistakes. This dream might be a sign that you know you've done something wrong, but are afraid to face the consequences of your actions.

SNAKES

Snakes tend to appear often in our dreams. The associations with them can vary from culture to culture, like any dream symbol, and with your own experiences with snakes as well. One common interpretation is that snakes symbolize the shedding of old habits, emotions, or beliefs. In this sense, the snake represents transformation. Just like a snake sheds its skin, this dream might be a sign for you to let go of the old and allow your new or renewed self to surface. These changes don't have to be frightening, but instead you should see them as an opportunity for positive growth that has come your way. Snakes can also be a symbol for fear. A snake on the hunt lies in wait, calculating carefully before striking out with sudden speed at its prey. In this case, you might be waiting in anxious anticipation of something. Perhaps you are afraid of the things in your life that are most unpredictable, or there are people in your life that you mistrust and fear will turn on you when you least expect it.

Sometimes, snakes symbolize temptation. This is more likely in cultures that are very familiar with the creation story of Adam and Eve, in which the snake, or serpent, is associated with both allure and evil. The snake in your dream could then be bringing your awareness to a situation in your waking life where you are being pressured into doing the wrong thing or betraying your values, so you may need to be on guard if you wish to protect yourself from a bad influence. Some other associations with snakes can include healing and creativity. Examine your waking life and your most immediate feelings about the snake to determine what interpretation is the most appropriate for your situation.

SPIDERS

Seeing spiders in your dream can be a little unsettling, but as a dream symbol, spiders actually aren't always negative. Spiders are creators, so they are associated with innovation, productivity, diligence, and feminine power, but they can be connected to lies or difficult (sticky) situations, too. On a positive note, spiders might embody your own desire to create. Maybe it is taking up a craft or hobby or studying music or painting. Just like spiders put time and care into building their beautiful, complicated webs, it may be time for you to take your own creative efforts more seriously and execute them with the diligence of a spider.

You might also think of a spider dream in terms of the phrase "a web of lies," since the symbols in your dreams can often be interpreted through metaphors. Are you really being honest with yourself and with others in your waking life? Are you being true to yourself? You might be feeling like you've put yourself in a situation that you can't get out of, which might be creating some anxiety in your waking life.

BEARS

Bears might seem scary in a dream, but they represent your inner nature and strength. They signify the untamed spirit of the dreamer and symbolize a need for more independence. If you're being chased by a bear in your dream, it might represent some kind of competition in your real life. A bear can also be an indicator that you are feeling like you are under attack in some way, which often will not be literal. Perhaps if one of your teachers seems to be extra critical of your reports and papers, a bear might show up in your dream!

BIRDS

Birds are a symbol of the imagination, hopes and dreams, independence, and ambition. They are almost always a positive sign when they appear in your dreams. Birds are often seen as cheery creatures, singing and flitting from branch to branch, so you might take this dream symbol as a sign of your own positivity and lightheartedness. You probably feel like you have the freedom to explore and express yourself in your waking life, and you aren't tied down by negative emotions or too many big responsibilities.

You don't let the pessimism of others bring down your mood and have confidence in your ability to reach the goals you have set for yourself. Birds may also represent your desire to be more like that.

LIONS

A lion in your dreams is a very good sign that you have healthy self-esteem. Lion dreams can mean that you are or will become a leader and have influence over the people around you. This can also mean that you feel loved and supported by your family, friends, and at school.

HORSES

Horses are symbolic of power, strength, and endurance. Seeing a horse in your dream might be a sign of your own strength of character, and if you realize that you are in the position of rider in this dream, you are probably taking charge of your own destiny and feel empowered to make your own decisions. Wild horses are a sign of freedom and a lack of restraint—and perhaps even a deep craving for adventure—while a bridled horse might represent your desire for some guidance in your waking life. You might be seeking out the wisdom of a "rider" to tell you where to go. Horses are also herd animals, so another interpretation is that they are a symbol of your desire for community and friendship.

FISH

Since water is the element of emotion, having dreams about fish might be related to how you navigate your feelings in your waking life. Think about the ways fish travel through currents, streams, waterfalls, coves, etc. What were the fish in your dream doing? Did you dream of fish fighting their way upstream? Maybe you have been fighting your own emotions in your waking life. Catching a fish in your dream could represent some emotions that have surfaced recently or something new that you've brought into your life. If your dream fishing trip was successful, this could also be a sign that you have everything you need in life. On the flip side, you might be feeling out of place. Maybe you're overwhelmed with so many responsibilities that you feel like you're struggling to catch a breath. If you are getting over a recent breakup, having a dream about fish could be a reminder that there are plenty of fish in the sea and you will have other chances to find love or friendship again even if it hurts now.

QUIZ

TEST YOUR KNOWLEDGE!

Sue is having a dream about being naked at the shopping mall. What is the most likely interpretation of her dream?

A. Sue doesn't have enough clothes.

B. Sue goes to the shopping mall too often.

C. Sue is afraid of what other people think of her.

D. Sue has been feeling confused lately.

Last night, Antonio dreamed that he was driving a car, when suddenly the car started swerving out of control. What could this mean about his waking life?

A. Something feels out of control in Antonio's life.

B. Antonio is a bad driver.

C. Antonio should seek out more adventure in life.

D. Things in Antonio's life are distracting him.

Jayla had a dream that she became a superhero. What could that possibly say about her?

A. Jayla is smarter than other people.

B. Jayla is scared of facing a big challenge in her life.

C. Jayla is confident in her own abilities.

D. Jayla has a lot of responsibilities.

Heewon recently had a dream that her girlfriend kissed someone else. This probably means that:

A. Heewon's girlfriend has been cheating on her.

B. Heewon feels insecure about her relationship.

C. Heewon wants to break up with her girlfriend.

D. Heewon is being too clingy.

Julian keeps dreaming about being trapped in quicksand. Which interpretation is the most likely?

A. Julian is letting his emotions get the better of him.

B. Julian misses going to the beach.

C. Julian is taking charge in his waking life.

D. Something is making Julian feel helpless.

Carter is having a dream that they are being chased by zombies. What might this mean?

A. Carter is too focused on following the crowd.

B. Someone in Carter's life has betrayed them.

C. Carter is becoming aggressive toward others.

D. Carter doesn't care what people think about them.

Answer Key: C, A, C, B, D, A

IF YOU ANSWERED 5 OR MORE CORRECTLY . . . YOU ARE A MASTER. Excellent work! You are now a master dream interpreter!

IF YOU ANSWERED 3 TO 4 CORRECTLY . . . YOU ARE A SCHOLAR. Great job! You have learned a lot and now you're ready to share your knowledge.

IF YOU ANSWERED 2 OR FEWER CORRECTLY . . . YOU ARE AN APPRENTICE. You're getting there! A little more study and soon you'll be able to interpret dreams with confidence!

INDEX

ABOUT THE AUTHOR
AND ILLUSTRATOR

CERRIDWEN GREENLEAF is the author of the bestselling Witch's Spellbook series. She has worked with many of the leading lights of the spirituality world and relies on her background in medievel studies to inform her work.

KHOA LE is an illustrator, graphic designer, and author based in Ho Chi Minh City, Vietnam. She is the illustrator of the RP Kids picture book *Sugar In Milk*. Khoa has also participated in art exhibitions throughout Vietnam and Asia. She currently lives with her four cats. She has a passion for traveling and discovering different cultures and art.